green guide

SHARKS
& RAYS

....

OF AUSTRALIA

Kelvin Aitken
Series Editor: Louise Egerton

NEW
HOLLAND

First published in 1998 by
New Holland Publishers (Australia) Pty Ltd
Sydney • Auckland • London • Cape Town

1/66 Gibbes Street Chatswood NSW 2067 Australia
218 Lake Road Northcote Auckland New Zealand
The Chandlery Unit 11450 Westminster Bridge Road London SE17QY
Wembley Square First Floor Solan Road Gardens Cape Town 8001 South Africa

Reprinted in 2003, 2005, 2007 and 2014

Series Editor: Louise Egerton
Project Manager: Fiona Doig
Designer: Laurence Lemmon-Warde
Cover design: Peta Nugent
Reproduction: DNL Resources
Printed and bound by Everbest, China

National Library of Australia Cataloguing-in-Publication Data:

Aitken, Kelvin
Sharks and rays of Australia
Includes index

ISBN 9781864363180

1. Sharks—Australia. 2. Sharks—Australia—Identification.
3. Rays (Fishes)—Australia 2. Rays (Fishes)—Australia—Identification. I. Title
(Series: Green guide).

597.30994

Photographic Acknowledgments

Photograph positions: t = top, b = bottom, c = centre, m = main, i = inset, l = left, r = right.

All photographs by **Kelvin Aitken** with the exception of the following: **Paul Baumann**: p. 64b;
CSIRO/Aitken: p. 36; **Saul Gonor**: p. 58; **Ken Hoppen**: p. 13, 35t, 42t, 60b, 84, 85t;
Rudie Kuiter: p. 74, 91t, 93i; **Mary Molloy**: p. 59i, 76i; **Kim & Allan Payard**: p. 75i;
Doug Perrine/Auscape: p. 51; **Becca Saunders/Twilight Zone**: pp. 56–57, p. 67t&i, pp. 70–71;
Roger Swainston: p. 62; **Dave Warth**: p. 37b.

CONTENTS

An Introduction to Sharks and Rays

Like all sharks, this Bronze Whaler shark differs from fish primarily because its skeleton is made of cartilage, not bone.

*T*his guide has been written with the amateur naturalist in mind, whether an angler, diver, snorkeler or wader. Australia is the shark and ray capital of the world and has far more different species of these animals than any other country. Of the 950 known species of sharks and rays, Australia is host to about 300; many of them are found only in our waters. Since the majority of Australians live clustered along the eastern and southern seaboard and we are such a beach- and sun-loving culture, we have a wonderful opportunity to both see these mysterious animals and to discover how they live.

How Sharks and Rays are Classified

Scientists divide all life on Earth, from the single-celled bacteria to trees to whales, into five large groups called 'kingdoms'. These, in turn, are divided up into smaller groups, each of which is called a 'phylum'. Sharks, rays and chimaeras are all types of fish and fish belong to the kingdom Animalia in the phylum Chordata. Chordata means animals with a backbone or spinal cord.

Fish are then further divided into one of four 'classes'. The main class of fish, the Osteichthyes, have a skeleton of bone but sharks, rays and chimaeras belong to another class of fish called chondrichthyans that have a skeleton made of cartilage. Cartilage is a gristly substance similar to

The spectacular Elephant Fish is a chimaera. Most chimaeras are restricted to deep water and are rarely seen.

Despite the shark-like tail and fins, the pectoral fins joined to the head indicate that this is a ray.

the supporting structure in your ears, nose or throat. Unlike other fish species, male chondrichthyans also have claspers, which are external reproductive organs. The other two small classes of fish are the lampreys and the hagfishes.

Sharks differ from rays and chimaeras in having 5–7 gills visible on the sides of the head and pectoral fins that are not joined to the head. They also have an upper jaw that is not fused to the skull. Rays have their pectoral fins or 'wings' joined to the head and gill slits underneath, not on the sides, of the head. Chimaeras have the upper jaw fused to the skull and have only one gill opening on each side of the head.

Shark Shock
Of all the animals on Earth, sharks seem to elicit the most negative emotional response from normally sane people. For so long we have been led to believe that all sharks are dangerous and that our lives are constantly at risk from these 'flesh-eating monsters'. The truth is rather different and much more fascinating.

WORDS TO KNOW
Abyssal plain: seabed below 2000 m.
Barbel: sensory tentacle.
Bycatch: animals caught unintentionally, usually discarded.
Clasper: male sex organs.
Continental slope: seabed from 200–2000 m.
Filament: like a thread.
Fusiform: spindle shaped, like a torpedo.
Gutter: corridor or passage in the reef.
Keel: a ridge of flesh or cartilage.
Nictitating eyelids: clear movable eyelid.
Pelagic: living in the open sea.
Spine: a sharp spike, usually serrated.
Thorns: spiky projections.
Trawl: net dragged behind a boat.

How do Sharks, Rays and Chimaeras Move?

A shark's primary means of locomotion is its tail or caudal fin. Because it is shaped to displace much water, it is often very large.

*T*hree basic methods of loco-motion are employed by this group. All sharks, and some rays like the shovelnose rays, use their tails as the main means of moving through water — just as many fish do. This may be augmented by the movement of their bodies as they sinuously push through the water. Some sharks, as well as some small reef fish, have been seen to swim fairly effectively when their tails have been removed, using only their body motion.

Rays use their wings to swim. Some, such as devilrays and eaglerays, beat these up and down in order to 'fly' through the water just like a bird. Others, like the stingrays and stingarees, create a wave-like motion along the edge of their wings that effectively pulls them through the water.

Chimaeras employ a third method of locomotion. They use their large pectoral fins like oars to scull through the water.

Where do Sharks, Rays and Chimaeras Live?

*S*harks, rays and chimaeras live in the world's oceans and coastal areas. Some sharks and rays even live in fresh water. The Bull Shark, for example, has been found 4000 km up the Amazon River of South America and also migrates up river to Lake Nicaragua.

Many sharks, rays and chimaeras live in very restricted depths or geographic zones. For example, the Epaulette Shark is only found on shallow tropical reefs, the Mitotic Stingaree has only been found in a small area off Port Headland and the Ogilbys Ghostshark is found only in waters 120–350 m deep off south-eastern Australia.

On the other hand some sharks, rays and chimaeras migrate long distances or have wide distribution. For example the Blue Shark has been tracked crossing hemispheres and across entire oceans. Cookie Cutter Sharks migrate vertically: from depths of 1000 m to the surface each night to feed. The widely distributed Manta Ray and Shortspine Spookfish can be found in the three main oceans around the world.

How Many Species are There?

*T*here are 950 known species of sharks, rays and chimaeras around the world. This makes up about 5 per cent of all known fish species.

In Australia the last comprehensive study estimated 166 species of sharks, 117 species of rays and 13 chimaeras in our waters. Of those only about 75 species would regularly be seen by swimmers and another 75 by trawlers.

The Whitetip Reef Shark is one of 166 Australian shark species.

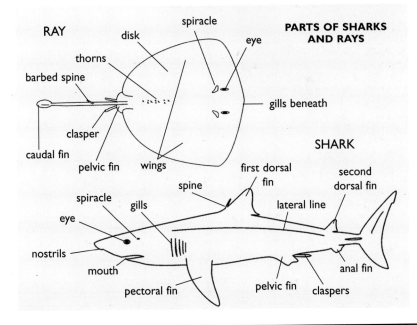

RAY

spiracle
disk
thorns
barbed spine
eye
clasper
caudal fin
pelvic fin
wings
gills beneath

PARTS OF SHARKS AND RAYS

SHARK

spiracle
gills
eye
nostrils
mouth
pectoral fin
spine
first dorsal fin
lateral line
second dorsal fin
anal fin
pelvic fin
claspers

HORN SHARKS

Who are the Horn Sharks?

Horn sharks are the most commonly seen sharks in southern waters; they are often found in small groups.

*H*orn sharks are a group of sharks that get their name from the sturdy spine in front of each dorsal fin. They are found in the subtropical to temperate seas of the Indian and Pacific Oceans.

Of the eight species, three can be found in Australia: the Port Jackson Shark, the Crested Horn Shark and the Zebra Horn Shark. The last is mostly an Asian species, although it is found also in the deep waters off northwestern Australia. Horn sharks forage for their food at night and are considered harmless.

How Fast can Sharks Swim?

*N*ot all sharks are fast swimmers. If hard pressed, they can outswim a snorkeler finning along at 3-5 knots but not for long as their metabolism is only suited to short bursts of speed. Some deep-water sharks are considered to be downright sluggish, merely hovering or slowly sculling along. Bottom-dwelling sharks from shallow waters, such as Port Jackson, Draughtboard or Blind Sharks, spend most of their time resting on the bottom and only move around slowly at night

The sleek streamlined bodies of many sharks allow them to reach high speeds over short distances.

foraging in the nooks and crannies of the reef.

The sharks that live in the open ocean must be much faster in order to catch their prey, such as speedy tuna or swordfish. The fastest shark is the Mako; with an in-water speed of 30-40 km per hour, it can leap 6 m or more above the surface. Migrating sharks have been measured travelling at about 3 km per hour but the normal daily swimming speed of a reef shark is estimated to be around 1 km per hour, with occasional bursts of speed when feeding.

What are Fins For?

*F*ins are used to propel, steady and steer. Sharks cannot swim backwards as their propulsion comes almost entirely from the tail. Most sharks have asymmetrical tails, with the upper lobe longer than the lower one but the open-ocean swimmers, such as the Mako and Great White Sharks, have nearly symmetrical tails, giving them more thrust.

The side-to-side movement of the tail or caudal fin is counteracted by the dorsal fins, which help to prevent roll, much like the keel on a yacht. The pectoral fins are used to travel on an even plane and, just like the flaps on an aeroplane, can be tilted and twisted to soar, roll or break forward momentum; a handy feature when feeding among rocks or coral. Pelvic and anal fins are useful to streamline and steady the body while swimming.

This shark lives in the open sea; its huge arched pectoral fins help it to coast like a glider and thereby aid in maintaining its buoyancy.

Who has the Biggest Fins?

*I*f you count the tail as a fin, the shark that has the largest fin in relation to its overall body size is the Thresher Shark. Its tail is about as long as its body. The gentle Zebra Shark runs a close second with its long paddle-shaped tail. The Oceanic Whitetip Shark has the longest and largest pectoral fins in relation to its size but for just plain enormous the Whale Shark has the biggest fins of any shark.

The thrust from the huge tail of this Zebra Shark is balanced and controlled by the other large paddle-shaped fins on its body.

SHARK FIN SOUP
Shark fins have an internal structure made up of rods of cartilage. These rods are bound together to provide the fin with both strength and flexibility. It is these rods that are extracted from a shark's fin to make shark fin soup.

Port Jackson Shark

The harness-shaped pattern is unique to Port Jackson Sharks (above). A Port Jackson Shark's egg case (left).

This is one of the most common sharks seen in southern waters, especially in New South Wales. The species ranges from southern Queensland around the southern States to Geraldton in Western Australia. Port Jacksons have a distinctive bulky, blunt head with a 'pursed' mouth. They are usually grey in colour with tints of brown or green, and a black-banded pattern on the body similar in shape to the harness worn by a seeing-eye dog.

Female Port Jackson Sharks may travel as far as 850 km to lay their eggs among shallow rocky reefs during late winter and spring. These spiral-shaped eggs are a dark green or brown when new but soon become almost black and encrusted with spots of algae. Females will sometimes push the eggs into crevices but often they will be wedged in by wave action. Eggs that have been left in the open or torn loose by storms are often found washed ashore. The young pups that hatch 10–12 months later are about 15–20 cm long at first but they grow to 1.5 m or more.

Nocturnal Feeders

Divers and snorkelers may come across Port Jackson Sharks, sometimes in groups of 10–20, lying in sheltered caves or gullies on shallow rocky reefs during the day. Here they sleep or rest until the night when they disperse to feed on sea urchins and shells. Their scientific name, *Heterodontus*, means 'different teeth' and refers to their spiky front teeth, which are ideal for prying and holding; the fused teeth-plates at the rear are perfectly developed for crushing shelled molluscs.

Crested Horn Shark

The yellowish brown colouring and prominent eye crests distinguish the Crested Horn Shark.

The Crested Horn Shark is only found on the east coast of Australia in a confined region from southern Queensland to Montague Island. Similarities with the Port Jackson are their teeth, diet and body shape. It can be best distinguished from the Port Jackson Shark by the larger crests above the eye and the lack of a harness-shaped pattern on the body, having two indistinct dark bands or 'saddles' over a yellowish brown base colour instead. They also have rounder dorsal fins and do not congregate in groups.

Tying up Egg Cases

Reproductive behaviour is very different from that of the Port Jackson Shark. Females lay spiral-shaped egg cases with long sticky tendrils up to 2 m long. The female chooses a section of reef, often where other females have already deposited their eggs, and tightly circles a suitable vertical projection, such as sea tulips, kelp or a rock. As she rubs her body against the reef the sticky tendrils, which have emerged slightly from her body, become attached, pulling out the egg cases as she swims away. The eggs are anchored to the reef by the well-tangled tendrils. Eight months later the 20–22 cm young emerge. They will grow to their adult size of 1.5 m.

LULLING DOCILE SHARKS

Horn sharks can be sent into a state of trance-like ecstasy by gently scratching their bellies and throats. However these docile sharks should not be handled as their robust dorsal spines can inflict a painful wound and their crushing teeth can mash a wayward finger.

CARPET SHARKS

Who are the Carpet Sharks?

*C*arpet sharks are a large group of bottom-dwelling sharks that have both pelvic and anal fins plus two dorsal fins but with no fin spines. They have a mouth just under or at the front of their short snout and on the inside edges of each nostril they have a barbel, which is a tentacle-like sensory growth. All carpet sharks have teeth to hold or crush fish, crabs and shelled molluscs except for the Whale Shark, which is an open-ocean plankton eater.

A short snout with barbels on the nostrils identifies all carpet sharks.

Are all Sharks Dangerous?

*W*hile some species can cause injury if provoked, of the world's 370 or more species only four are considered truly dangerous. These are the Tiger Shark, the Bull Shark, the Oceanic Whitetip Shark and the Great White Shark. Today, with greater knowledge of the biology of sharks, what triggers attack behaviour, feeding strategies, preferred food and territorial behaviour, we can dive safely in open water with all but the Great White Shark.

The Great White Shark, with its massive size and bold manner, is best filmed and observed from protective cages. Even so, most chance encounters with this

species seem to be more a matter of the shark making a curious inspection rather than an attack. Statistically there is more chance of dying from a bee sting, a bolt of lightning, drowning or a drive to the beach than from a shark attack but, like any wild animal, a shark's defence or attack mechanisms need to be treated with a considerable amount of respect.

This Great White Shark's feeding instincts have been aroused by bait; such sharks are best observed by divers from the security of a cage.

Why do some Sharks Attack?

*H*umans are not part of a shark's diet so for many years researchers have tried to find out what causes the occasional shark attack. All attacks can be attributed to two main causes: defence and food.

Spearing, netting, catching on a line and harassing sharks are rightly interpreted by the shark to be attacks and to these they will react defensively. Like humans, they often

The impressive teeth of a threatened shark are understandably used as a primary means of defence.

react strongly and often without thinking to surprise attacks; for example, if we are grabbed from behind we are likely to react violently. Some sharks are also territorial, like the Grey Reef Shark, and they may try to defend their territory from other large animals, such as divers.

Almost all of the shark's sensory system is used to find, catch and consume food. When berley (usually a minced mix of fish meat and oil) or bait is used to attract fish, sharks are also attracted. Attacks on spearfishers and fishing boats can be attributed to a shark following its senses to a food source. Also some sharks feed on schooling fish at the surface, so they may confuse the splashing of swimmers or surfers with struggling prey.

Are Sharks Intelligent?

*R*esearchers have conducted experiments that show that at least some species of shark can be trained to operate equipment to obtain a reward. Some dive operations organise regular weekly or monthly shark dives and in some places the sharks have learned to recognise the noise of the boat and travel to the dive site to be fed on proffered baits while ignoring the divers.

A shark cage with divers submerges for these curious adventurers to view Great White Sharks.

Varied Carpet Shark

Since it relies on camouflage, this shark is easy to approach and instantly identified by the white speckles on its black collar.

Common along the coasts of all southern States, the Varied Carpet Shark is found in both deep and shallow water. It often snoozes in sheltered crevices of a rocky reef or among seagrasses and is more active at night, when it forages among reefs and weeds for worms, crustaceans and molluscs. It crushes their shells in its small mouth. Scattered across its grey to brown body are white spots and on its fins, black blotches.

Rusty Carpet Shark

Like many carpet sharks, Rusty Carpet Sharks rest and hide among bottom growth during the day.

The Rusty Carpet Shark differs from the Varied Carpet Shark in its colour pattern. It lacks the pitch black collar with the dense white spots. Instead it has a hazy or indistinct collar patch matched by five or six hazy 'saddles' or broad bands down its body. It has brown instead of white spots on the body and fins with a base colour of grey or brown fading into a paler tone on the belly.

Like the Varied Carpet Shark the female Rusty Carpet Shark lays small eggs during winter and early spring with tendrils that attach them to reef vegetation. Distribution is from the eastern Victorian border around to Albany in Western Australia. It can be found in the shallows by snorkelers but is normally encountered by scuba divers at depths of more than 15 m on densely carpeted reefs or, at times, on deep seagrass beds. All carpet sharks are harmless but react violently when handled.

Blind Shark

The Blind Shark can be found from Morton Bay down to southern New South Wales. In colour it is light to very dark chocolate brown with small white specks on the back and flanks. Juveniles have a series of distinct dark bands on the body that fade and disappear as they reach adulthood. The body is chubby with a broad head sporting obvious barbels on

The Blind Shark uses its long nasal barbels to help it locate food among weed and sand.

the nostrils. There is a large spiracle behind each eye, which allows the shark to grub about in silty areas without disturbing its breathing.

Blind Sharks are nocturnal. They rest in caves, ledges or sheltered crevices during the day. At night they feed on various invertebrates, such as crabs and shelled invertebrates, as well as small fish. Blind Sharks are often found in heavy surge zones where rock fishermen occasionally land a specimen. When caught they close their eyes, a habit which gives them their common name.

Brown Banded Bamboo Shark

This tropical species is found across the northern coast of Australia. Its common name comes from the juvenile's pattern of dark chocolate brown bands on a cream body; these blend and fade to a uniform grey or brown in adulthood. When the young hatch from their eggs they are about 17 cm long but they grow to a metre or more. Their bodies are slender with broad paddle-shaped pectoral fins that are used to wedge themselves into crevices to avoid predators. This shark is often con-fused with the Nurse or Blind Shark

The dark bands on juvenile Bamboo sharks fade to pale saddles when they reach adulthood.

but it can be easily distinguished by the conspicuous white edges to its gills.

While the Brown Banded Bamboo Shark may occur at depths as great as 90 m, it is far more common in shallow reef areas where it feeds on inverte-brates, such as crabs and shelled molluscs, as well as small fish. This shark has the ability to live for extended periods out of water. This enables it to survive quite comfortably when it becomes stranded in rock pools at low tide.

Zebra Shark

The zebra-like stripes of young Zebra Sharks change to spots when they become adults.

The very distinctive Zebra Shark has a tail second in proportional length only to that of the Thresher Shark. Hard ridges run down the back and flanks. The head is short and rounded with small eyes and a mouth close to the tip of the snout. The dark brown to black juveniles with yellowish white bars and spots give this shark its common name. As it grows to adulthood the bars are replaced by a mosaic of dark brown spots on a yellowish to dark brown base colour; this coloration gives rise to its other common name, Leopard Shark.

TAKING ADVANTAGE OF CURRENTS

Like all bottom-dwelling sharks, Zebra Sharks have the ability to pump water over their gills, either through the mouth or through the large spiracle behind each eye. During the day they can be found resting in current-prone areas facing the flow to make breathing a less stressful chore. Even though a diver will only see four gill openings, there are, in fact, five gills, with two sharing the one opening.

Life Cycle and Companions

The 17 cm long egg cases of the Zebra Shark are festooned with golden hair-like tufts that catch on the reef. The hatchlings, 20 cm long, grow to at least 2.5 m. This docile shark can be approached very closely. It is common to see remoras clinging to its belly and sides or small disc-shaped parasites around its mouth.

Epaulette Shark

The common name for this shark comes from the large dark spot that develops over each pectoral fin of the adults, much like the epaulette shoulder patches on a military uniform. Juveniles have dark 'saddles' on the back that fade as the speckled adult coloration takes over. Epaulette Sharks are egg-layers with juveniles 15 cm long growing to an

This distinctively patterned Epaulette Shark is often found foraging in coral reef shallows.

adult size of one metre. The distinctive colour pattern easily distinguishes this shark from other similar-shaped carpet sharks.

Epaulette Sharks are commonly found in tropical Australian waters and are the most accessible of all sharks for reef waders and snorkelers. During the day they hide under ledges and large sections of coral rubble, at times in just a few inches of water. During the night they can be found in the shallows foraging for small invertebrates. This shark is harmless and will happily go about its business among waders if not harassed.

Tawny Nurse Shark

This is a common shark in tropical waters. Coloured grey to sandy brown, it can change its tone slightly depending on the colour of its environment, an ability that other sharks, like the Port Jackson, also have. This is a large shark, growing from a length of 40 cm at birth to reach over 3 m. Its broad, flattened head with squarish snout, tiny eyes and large fins make it a distinctive

Most Tawny Nurse Sharks, such as this juvenile, are found during the day in caves.

animal. At a casual glance it may be confused with the notorious Tiger Shark but the long tail and large dorsal fins set well towards the rear define this docile species.

The Tawny Nurse Shark's common name is derived from its ability to suck up prey using a powerful sucking motion with its throat, just like a baby being nursed. This talent is used to vacuum out octopuses, fish and crabs from the reef or it can be reversed to fire a jet of water at any captor.

Do all Sharks Lay Eggs?

*A*ll sharks originate as eggs in the ovaries of the female. What happens after conception varies depending on the species. There are three basic strategies of reproduction.

The first, called oviparity, is when the young hatch from an egg laid by the mother. The second, viviparity, is when the young develop within the mother, forming a placental connection in the uterus similar to human and mammalian reproduction. These young are born as living independent individuals and are almost identical in appearance to their parents.

The third strategy, ovoviviparity, is a combination of the two former strategies. This is when the female has eggs that hatch inside the body but where no placental connection takes place. The embryos of these types of sharks live off their yolk sac for most of their time in the uterus but, as this becomes depleted, they begin to absorb nutrients that are secreted from the uterus walls until their birth.

Many egg-laying sharks use sticky tendrils to attach their eggs to bottom growth.

The Egg-layers

*O*viparous sharks lay eggs containing an embryo that feeds off a yolk in the same way as birds or reptiles. Unlike other fish species that produce enormous batches, allowing for high mortality rates of both eggs and juveniles, sharks only produce a few eggs. These eggs have rugged but flexible casings, often referred to as 'mermaid's purses', that come in a variety of shapes and sizes. Many have tendrils or special membranes that either anchor themselves on reefs or catch on the seabed by means of ribs and ridges. Sometimes they become camouflaged by algal growth, thereby reducing their susceptibility to discovery by predators. Sometimes, however, the egg cases wash up on beaches, especially after storms. If the embryo develops without mishaps, the young shark hatches out of the egg case and begins its life in the ocean, sometimes with a camouflage pattern very different from that of the adult.

Despite their tough exterior, egg cases can absorb water and oxygen at latter stages of the embryos growth.

Do Sharks have Nests?

Some sharks may deposit their eggs in one location but they are not placed in a constructed nest, like those of birds, and there is no care of the eggs and resulting hatchlings. Sharks' eggs are left to the whims of the environment. The embryos develop, hatch and begin life without any parental nurturing. At times large numbers of eggs are found in a single small area: this is because a number of females have chosen it as a suitable laying site.

BABY CANNIBALS

A few of the viviparous sharks employ a form of cannibalism that occurs in the uterus. The first embryo to develop begins to consume the other eggs or embryos as they come into the uterus. This cannibalistic behaviour is called oviphagous feeding. While the mother may produce many eggs and embryos, only the largest and strongest survive.

What is the World's Most Common Shark?

The White-Spotted Spurdog or Piked Dogfish is possibly the most common shark found around the world. However in Australia it is only found off parts of the southern coast. The Blue Shark has the widest distribution in Australia and the world, being found in all oceans from the coasts of Alaska and Norway down to the Falkland Islands.

In certain confined areas some species are very common: the Brier Shark, which lives in deep waters, for example, is found in large numbers in commercial fishing areas and Gummy Sharks, Grey Nurse Sharks and Grey Reef Sharks are common in certain areas during their breeding seasons.

The sleek Blue Shark has an unmatched worldwide distribution, being found in all oceans.

Ornate Wobbegong

The blotchy disruptive pattern of the Ornate Wobbegong provides excellent camouflage.

All wobbegongs have a flattened body shape and fleshy lobes or tassels of skin around the head and jaws. Of the six Australian species, the Ornate Wobbegong has the widest distribution. Commonly found resting among rocky or coral reefs, this species can be confused with the similar patterns of the Spotted Wobbegong but it has dark blotches and 'saddles' edged in black spots while the Spotted Wobbegong has dark blotches and 'saddles' edged in white spots.

WOUNDING BY WOBBEGONG

If a wobbegong is molested or attacked, its spear-shaped holding teeth can inflict a painful but shallow wound. Care should be taken when wading or diving in the vicinity of wobbegongs as their perfect camouflage can trick the unwary, an excuse unacceptable to the grumpy wobbegong.

Sit-and-Wait Hunters

While wobbegongs tend to be more active at night, they are opportunistic feeders taking a meal at any time that suits their cantankerous disposition. Their hunting technique is a sit-and-wait strategy that relies on their superb camouflage to trick fish, lobsters, octopuses and cuttlefish that wander into their range. At times they may also prop themselves up on their pectoral fins and hold their heads high to attract prey to their tassels. When a victim comes into range a lightening fast snap of the jaws secures the prey, which is swallowed whole. Large prey items may be held for days in a bulldog grip until dying, allowing the wobbegong to swallow its victim without a struggle.

Spotted Wobbegong

The Spotted Wobbegong is commonly found in temperate waters. At times small groups can be found resting together in caves or ledges. A distinctive small triangle between the eyes is unique to this species. Like all wobbegongs, the Spotted Wobbegong gives birth to live young that have hatched out of eggs within the uterus. The newborn pups are 20 cm long and grow to an adult size of 3 m or more.

A triangular pattern between the eyes clearly identifies the Spotted Wobbegong.

Spotted Wobbegongs have been targeted by New South Wales fisheries, their meat being used for the fish-and-chip trade. As a result reefs once littered with Spotted Wobbegongs now shelter only the occasional individual. Adding to this species' economic viability is the fact that its hide makes an attractive leather.

Normally placid, the Spotted Wobbegong can become aggressive if tempted with bait, such as speared fish or scraps from cleaned fish. A wobbegong should never be harassed by grabbing its tail as it can easily turn and bite within its own body length.

Tasselled Wobbegong

This species is found only in tropical waters. It has a distinctive mass of lobes and tendrils around the jaws, more so than any other wobbegong species. The scientific name for the Tasselled Wobbegong, *Eucrossorhinus dasypogon*, roughly translates into 'well fringed nose with shaggy beard'. It has a very broad head, large spiracles set behind small eyes, large rounded pectoral fins and a beautiful mosaic pattern of spots and lines all over a yellowish brown body.

Like all wobbegongs, the Tasselled Wobbegong relies on camouflage and quick reflexes to snatch prey that strays too close to its head. Of course, the lush beard adds another dimension to its hunting with the frilly tassels appearing to be succulent morsels that attract fish, squid, cuttlefish and crabs. Its very flexible flattened body shape allows it to squirm into enclosed spaces or manoeuvre in caves for the best hunting spots.

Lush worm-like tassels on the snout attract prey towards the patient Tasselled Wobbegong's mouth.

Which Shark is the Largest?

Snorkelers are dwarfed by the mass of this average-sized Whale Shark.

*T*he Whale Shark is not only the largest shark in the world, it is also the largest living fish in the oceans. It grows 12–18 m long or more and weighs up to 1 tonne per metre.

The Whale Shark is the only member in its family and very little is known about it. Only recently has the first pregnant female been examined to find that they are ovoviviparous; that is they have egg cases within the uterus but give birth to live young. The juveniles, born at about 60 cm long, are released from the mother in their hundreds.

Eggs released by coral spawning attract schools of small fish, creating a feast for migrating Whale Sharks.

Whale Sharks migrate over large areas throughout all tropical oceans and have been found as far south as Tasmania. Large groups of mostly immature males are found each year during autumn off the coast of central Western Australia. Here they feed on schools of small fish that thrive on the annual coral spawning, which occurs after the full moon in March to May.

Are Whale Sharks Whales?

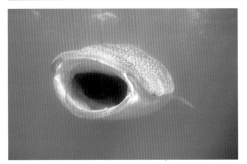

When feeding, the cavernous mouth of a Whale Shark could accommodate an object the size of a small car.

*W*hale Sharks are sharks and not whales. Whales are warm-blooded mammals that suckle their young and breath air but Whale Sharks, like all fish, absorb oxygen from the water through their gills; they do not suckle their young and are not warm blooded. Their name is derived from their whale-like proportions.

A Gentle Giant

Despite its gigantean size, the gentle Whale Shark is a harmless giant that feeds on plankton and small fish. It collects its food from near the surface of the ocean by swimming with its enormous mouth open. As the water passes through the gills the food is retained by sieve-like gill rakers.

Whale Sharks do possess an enormous number of teeth — 300 rows in each jaw — but they are tiny and at worst would only inflict a bad gravel rash. However divers and swimmers are warned to be careful when swimming with this shark as a collision with an animal of this size could cause injury.

Which is the Smallest Shark?

*T*he smallest shark known to humans is the Smalleye Pygmy Shark. The largest measured specimen was 22 cm long. This nocturnal feeder, found in Australian waters off New South Wales and Western Australia, migrates vertically from depths of 2000 m to within 200 m of the surface in its search for food. The underside of this tiny shark has luminous organs. The purpose of these may be to attract prey or to help it to blend in with the star- or moonlit surface and so avoid predators that are watching from below. Very little is known about the biology of the various pygmy sharks and so a still smaller contestant for the title of smallest shark may yet be found among this barely studied group.

Mackerel Sharks

Who are the Mackerel Sharks?

*M*ackerel sharks share a number of features with other groups of sharks, such as pelvic and anal fins, a mouth that extends back past their eyes, two dorsal fins without spines and five pairs of gills. They are most similar to the ground sharks but what separates them is the lack of a nictitating eyelid, which is a tough protective membrane that can be pulled over the eyes by a special muscle. Instead they are able to roll the eye up into the skull to protect it when feeding.

Mackerel sharks include harmless plankton feeders as well as the notorious Great White Shark.

Do Sharks get Cavities?

*S*harks replace their teeth so often that they do not get the chance to form cavities. Unlike mammals, sharks have a system of regular tooth replacement. Rows of developing teeth form on the internal surface of both jaws. As soon as a tooth is knocked out or broken the next tooth in line rolls forward to take its place. Letting nothing go to waste, Cookie Cutter Sharks swallow their teeth in order to supplement their calcium levels.

Juvenile sharks may replace individual teeth every seven or eight days while larger sharks may replace

In sharks, new teeth lie nestled inside the jaw ready to roll forward when the outer ones become dislodged.

their entire set over a year. Depending on species and longevity, a shark may shed 10 000–30 000 teeth in a lifetime, which explains why sharks' teeth are so common in the fossil record.

Assorted Tooth Styles

*T*he shape of shark's teeth varies between species according to what they eat and the lifestyles they lead. Bottom-dwelling sharks that feed on crabs and shells have crushing teeth or plates. Sharks that catch fast-swimming fish have long needle-like teeth to hold their prey. Sharks that feed on large animals have flat cutting teeth with serrated edges to slice through the tough skin and bone.

The narrow, pointy teeth of a Grey Nurse Shark (left) are used to hold prey, which is swallowed whole. The blade-like serrated teeth of a Tiger Shark (right) are used to slice large prey into smaller portions.

Some sharks may have two different types of teeth in their jaws. Others alter their tooth shape as they grow larger and feed on different prey. For example, in order for the Mako Shark to catch and consume fast pelagic fish, it begins life with narrow needle-shaped teeth but as it grows these become thicker and heavier to accommodate larger prey, such as dolphins and billfish.

How Hard can Sharks Bite?

*T*ests have been done to measure the bite strength of a shark. Although not indicative of all sharks under all feeding conditions, measurements taken from a small two-metre shark gave a reading of 60 kg for one tooth, which translates into 3 tonnes per square centimetre. Suffice it to say that a combination of weight and multiple razor sharp teeth will allow a large shark to easily decapitate a tuna or slice a seal in half, and bottom-dwellers can easily crush thick shells. To put this into perspective, our molar bite is measured at 90 kg per tooth but our teeth are relatively blunt so we must chew our food; sharks just tear and swallow.

BIG TOOTH

The largest individual teeth belong to the Great White Shark, with the tallest enamel height for a tooth recorded at 70 mm. The largest tooth size for any known shark is from an extinct *Megalodon*: this name means 'giant tooth' and from the tip of its tooth to the base of the enamel this shark's tooth measured a huge 115 mm.

A fossilised tooth of the extinct giant Megalodon shark. It is the largest tooth of any known shark species.

Grey Nurse Shark

The fierce-looking but inoffensive Grey Nurse Shark has dorsal fins of a similar size.

Based purely on its fearsome looks this shark was once blamed for most shark attacks on humans and was hunted and fished to near extinction. Today the docile Grey Nurse Shark enjoys protected status in some Australian States. It is the first shark in the world to be protected by law.

The small head of the Grey Nurse, with tiny glowering eyes and needle-sharp snaggle teeth protruding from a gaping mouth, is followed by an almost humped back with similar-sized dorsal, pelvic and anal fins. Its dark grey colour merges into pure white on the belly with small coin-sized brown spots on the flanks. The face and tail, with a long upper lobe, distinguish this species from others. Grey Nurse Sharks grow to 3.2 m.

Habitat and Habits

Grey Nurse Sharks can be found from the surface down to 200 m deep all around Australia (except Tasmania). They are normally seen during the day in sheltered gutters or caves where they hover almost motionless, due to their ability to swallow air at the surface that counteracts their natural tendency to sink. A sociable species, they often gather in small to huge schools of mixed sexes and sizes so closely that they appear to be stacked like a cord of wood.

Their social and curious nature allows divers to make close contact but they should not be cornered or harassed as they will bite with lightening speed if threatened. From a motionless hover they can accelerate instantly to catch fast-swimming kingfish or salmon, so fast in fact that their tail creates a cavity in the water causing a deep boom to be heard.

Great White Shark

The awesome Great White Shark has the bulk and power to feed regularly on large marine mammals.

The most notorious of all sharks is the Great White. The light to dark grey back fades to pale grey on the sides, with a bronzy sheen in certain light. The belly is white and the underside of the large pectoral fins may be dusky at the tips and/or have a dark spot near the body. This shark's conical snout is usually heavily scarred from the defences of its prey and the large eyes are pure black. The mouth remains partially open with the bottom teeth always visible and the tail is an almost symmetrical crescent shape.

Much Hype Based on Little Knowledge

For such a fearsome shark, it is perhaps surprising that no serious studies of this species have been undertaken until recently: not until 1985 was the first pregnant female reliably recorded. She had seven near-term embryos, each about one metre long and weighing 13 kg. Studies show that only the larger Great White Sharks regularly prey on marine mammals, such as seals and dolphins, their main diet consisting of fish, particularly tuna, and smaller sharks.

Great White Sharks are now protected in many countries, including some States of Australia. Their low birth rate has not kept up with the numbers being caught by sporting anglers and commercial fishing vessels and many are killed by nets set for other species.

> **TALL TALES**
> The maximum size for a Great White Shark is a subject of great controversy, with exaggeration being the yardstick. Despite stories of mythical Great Whites being 10 m long, the largest specimen reliably measured to date has been 6.4 m long.

Are all Sharks Cold-blooded?

*A*ll fish are considered to be cold blooded, meaning that their body temperature is just above the temperature of the surrounding environment. However recent research has shown that some sharks and other fish benefit from a heat exchange system that effectively raises their body temperature 5–8°C above the norm.

Fast-swimming sharks, such as the Mako, Great White Shark and also the thresher sharks, have two bands of red muscle running down their bodies. Blood that has been warmed as a consequence of red muscle contractions returns to the heart and gills. It travels past incoming blood that has been cooled and oxygenated by external water at the gills. Heat exchange occurs between the closely packed blood vessels.

While the temperature increase may seem only small, its effect is to increase the rate of the animal's chemical reactions by two or three times. This heat transfer mechanism produces a far more efficient use of oxygen, thereby increasing the animal's speed and endurance, accelerating its digestion and even increasing the performance of its brain and eyes, which must be used in a cold dark environment to find swift and elusive prey.

How do Sharks Breathe?

*S*harks extract oxygen from the water with their gills. Many species must keep moving in order to force water through their gills. Other sharks live sluggish lives on the bottom, such as the camouflaged angel sharks that are stationary ambush hunters. They use muscular contractions of their mouths and throats to force water through the spiracles behind each eye and in so doing they pump water over their gills.

Gills are closely packed, thin, frilled membranes, each with a blood supply. Oxygen replenishment in the blood is from seawater via the gills.

How Long do Sharks Live?

*S*harks have a long lifespan compared to other fish. The shark with the longest lifespan seems to be the Piked or White-spotted Dogfish, which reaches maturity at about 20 years of age and lives to be at least 70 years old. Lemon Sharks, which have been extensively studied in the Atlantic, live for at least 50 years and the common School Shark has a similar lifespan.

This mature School Shark may be well over 20 years old.

Most sharks live for 20–30 years while some smaller sharks live an estimated 10–15 years.

Growth rates vary considerably between species and even between individual animals of the same species. They can also vary dramatically depending on climate, environment and food supplies. Fast-growing sharks, such as the Blue Shark, the Mako Shark and the Great White Shark, add about 30 cm per year to their length while the slow-growing White-spotted Spurdog grows only by a mere 1.5–2 cm per year.

Do Sharks Sleep?

*O*pen-water sharks may become less active at certain times during their travels and other species may rest on the bottom where the current can sweep over their gills but sharks do not sleep as we do. When divers and anglers find sharks apparently asleep in gutters, it is usually in a spot where currents with high oxygen levels form, thereby permitting the sharks to fall into a trance-like state.

> **EASILY OVERFISHED**
> The long-lived White-spotted Spurdog not only takes many years to grow to a usable size, it also produces small litters that can take up to 2 years to be born after conception. Long lifespans, small litter sizes and slow growth rates make all sharks, and especially commercially hunted species, vulnerable to overfishing.

A typical reef ledge funnels strong currents over a resting shark, thus delivering an ample supply of oxygen to its gills.

Thresher Sharks

The unmistakable shape of the world's longest shark tail easily identifies the thresher sharks.

All three species of thresher shark are found in Australian waters. They are basically grey but tinted with a beautiful metallic sheen of blue, purple or violet. Their most notable feature is their tails, which make up half their body length. Each species lives in a different habitat.

FATAL TAIL SWIPES

The name 'thresher' comes from the method with which these sharks hunt. Using their long tails, they herd small baitfish or squid into a tight ball, then charge through the school or stun the fish with a swipe of the tail. The vertebrae at the tip of the tail are enlarged slightly to give extra weight to the blow. During the summer months thresher sharks are often sighted leaping above the surface as they feed.

The Three Threshers

The Bigeye Thresher Shark, which grows to 4.6 m, dwells at depths as great as 500 m in the open ocean. Its large eyes are situated near the top of its head so that it can easily spot overhead schools of fish or squid silhouetted against the surface light. The Common Thresher Shark (see map) is often caught close to shore but this shy animal is rarely seen by divers. With a maximum body length of 5.5 m and a small mouth only suited to feeding on small fish, it is considered harmless but anglers rightly respect the tail as a well-placed swipe can break bones. The Pelagic Thresher lives far offshore in tropical waters. Growing to just 3.5 m, it has a relatively short dorsal fin and a more slender body than other thresher species.

Mako Shark

A clear look at a Mako Shark quickly picks up the snaggle-toothed gape, long conical snout, large black eyes and the metallic indigo blue colour on the back fading down the sides to a white belly and a tail with almost symmetrical lobes. This species can be found anywhere off Australia except for the Gulf of Carpentaria.

Symmetrical tail lobes and muscular body give the Mako Shark enormous speed and power.

Anglers count the Mako as a prize catch since their fighting ability is enhanced by spectacular aerial leaps. It is feared to some extent around boats as it has been recorded attacking and damaging craft, an event possibly encouraged by berley and/or electrical fields sensed around metal in the water. On the other hand, Mako Sharks have been hand fed in the open by divers and there are no documented unprovoked attacks on humans. This fast-swimming shark eats speedy prey, such as tuna and billfish, with larger specimens also feeding on dolphins.

Basking Shark

Growing to 10 m, the Basking Shark is the world's second largest fish. This harmless giant is greyish brown in colour with a long snout, tiny eyes and gill slits that almost surround the head. The tail has a large upper lobe which, along with the dorsal fin, is often seen protruding above the surface.

Often mistaken for a giant Great White Shark by anglers, the harmless Basking Shark feeds on plankton.

Basking Sharks are seen during summer across the southern coast of Australia but sightings are rare, being more common in the Northern Hemisphere. A huge oily liver — about 25 per cent of their body weight — helps them to maintain neutral buoyancy. Their most notable feature is an enormous mouth, which is opened to allow plankton to be strained out through their huge arched gill slits. It is assumed that the gill rakers, which are frilled filters attached to the gill arches, are lost during the winter when they apparently hibernate in deep water. Despite being an important commercial species, we know virtually nothing about its life or breeding habits and this shark has been hunted close to extinction.

GROUND SHARKS

Who are the Ground Sharks?

*G*round sharks are the most numerous group of sharks, with about 200 different species accounted for, among them the famous whaler sharks and the hammerhead sharks. Whalers were named after their habit of feeding on dead whales harpooned from whaling ships. All ground sharks have nictitating eyelids; that is movable eyelids that slide up over the eye for protection while feeding or being attacked. All, too, have pointed teeth; crushing plates are absent.

Whaler sharks are a type of ground shark. The species are so similar they are difficult to identify.

What Preys on Sharks?

Larger invertebrates such as this Eleven-armed Sea Star will prey on smaller sharks.

*B*esides humans, the biggest predator of sharks are other sharks. Many species include smaller sharks in their diet. Killer Whales and gropers also eat sharks. Recently a 6 metre female Killer Whale was filmed killing a 3 metre Great White Shark, allowing her calf to feed on the liver.

Commercial fishing kills millions of sharks every year, either as targeted species or as an unwanted bycatch during fishing operations. Recreational fishing often targets sharks during tournaments or they become part of the bycatch. Overfishing of the shark's natural prey reduces shark numbers, as does pollution and coastal development.

Are some Sharks Poisonous?

*T*he flesh of some sharks carry such a high level of mercury that it can become dangerous when eaten repeatedly. Whitetip Reef Sharks have been known to give ciguatera poisoning, an affliction that effects the human nervous system. Symptoms include violent nausea, hot and cold sensations and tingling of the skin. In extreme cases ciguatera poisoning may lead to coma and death.

Sharks with spines can inflict a painful wound and some, such as the Piked Dogfish, have glands that inject venom into the wound, causing intense pain.

What Defences do Sharks Have?

*T*he skin of a shark is covered in a protective layer of tiny tooth-like denticles that serves as a type of tough flexible armour. Many species have spines in front of one or both dorsal fins which can deter large predators and teeth are used for both feeding and as a defensive weapon.

Often the first defence a shark will employ when attacked is to flee. Other passive reactions are employed by the swell sharks: their name comes from their ability to rapidly swallow water or air so as to inflate their stomachs when threatened or captured. This serves the purpose of making them look bigger to predators and it also helps them to wedge into the ledges or caves in which they are often found.

Many species of sharks have sharp spines in front of their dorsal fins for defence.

Camouflage: Best Form of Defence

All sharks, from the huge-spotted Whale Shark to the tiny black Pygmy Shark, employ some form of camouflage. Camouflage can conceal a shark from harm. The most prominent examples are the ambush hunters that have disruptive camouflage, such as the Tasselled Wobbegong or the finely spotted angel sharks, that imitate the sandy environment in which they hide. Many bottom-dwelling sharks hide in reefs.

Deep-water sharks are often dark brown or black. Lantern sharks even have luminous organs on their bellies to help them blend in with the faint surface light. Many sharks have countershading. This is where the back is dark — to blend in with the ocean when viewed from above — and the belly is white — to match

This Tasselled Wobbegong is so well camouflaged it is difficult to distinguish it from the similarly patterned background.

the surface when seen from below. When viewed from the side, the gradation of colour from the back to the belly is surprisingly effective in the way it enables the shark to blend easily into its oceanic setting.

Catsharks

The Grey Spotted Catshark (top) is found on the southeastern coast and the Draughtboard Shark (inset) is very common along the southern coast.

With over 100 species, catsharks form the largest family of sharks. The name comes from their cat-like eyes and slender shape. Despite their diversity, little is known about them. This is due partly to their nocturnal lifestyle and, in many cases, deep-water habitats — some species are found at depths of more than 2000 m.

Catsharks can be found in all Australian waters from the far northern tropics to the cold temperate zones south of Tasmania. It can be difficult to differentiate between species due to similarities in colouring and patterns, as well as overlapping ranges. They differ from the similar-looking dogfishes by having an anal fin and from the houndsharks by having the first dorsal fin, when viewed in profile, slightly over or behind the pelvic fins. These harmless sharks live on the seabed where they eat small fish and invertebrates.

Draughtboard Shark

The swell sharks — so named for their ability to blow themselves up like blimps — make up a large group within the catshark family and the most common species of swell shark encountered by anglers and divers is the harmless Draughtboard Shark. It is found in cool southern waters from New South Wales to Western Australia. Its brown to grey body is covered with dark blotches and spots that give it the appearance of a chessboard. The head is slightly flattened and the golden eyes are almond-shaped. The pectoral fins are large and two dorsal fins are set well back on the body. Draughtboard Sharks are often found squeezed into lobster pots where they have become caught while looking for food. Their pale ridged egg cases are often found attached to kelp or weed.

Hound Sharks

A silvery Gummy Shark (top) blends into murky water; School Sharks (inset) have a similar camouflage.

*M*ost members of the hound shark group are noted primarily for their commercial value. Varying in length from 80 cm to 1.7 m, members of this small harmless family bear most of the features of the more renowned whaler sharks but they lack a notch in front of the tail and there are internal differences, too. The main commercial species occur in inshore southern Australian waters; lesser-known species live in deeper offshore tropical water. All have a varied diet of small fish, squid, octopuses and crabs.

School and Gummy Sharks

Two familiar species are the School Shark and the Gummy Shark. Both make long migrations across the southern coastline — tagged Gummy Sharks have been tracked from Tasmania to Western Australia during breeding season.

When adult, the slender 1.3–1.8 m School Shark has a translucent nose and a beautiful large sculptured tail. Although found throughout southern Australia, these sharks are rarely seen by divers due to their timid nature: nearby fishermen may be pulling them in with no underwater sightings by the divers at all. School Sharks live for over 55 years, with females producing 15–50 pups only every third year once mature at 10 years of age. These factors make this shark susceptible to overfishing and they have indeed become so.

The Gummy Shark has also been heavily fished and is sold as 'flake'. It lives for about 16–17 years, with females over the age of five giving birth to an average of 14 pups. Despite its name, the Gummy Shark does have small bluntly pointed teeth, which are ideal for crushing its food of small fish, crabs, squid and octopus. While Gummy and School Sharks are very similar in shape and size, the former has a pattern of small white spots over a bronze-grey back and a distinctive lateral line.

Grey Reef Shark

The Grey Reef Shark can become aggressive if tempted with bait or if harassed.

Of the whaler sharks, the Grey Reef Shark is one of the most common species found on tropical coral reefs. Despite only growing to 1.8 m long, it is one to be respected due to its territorial and assertive behaviour. Many studies have been undertaken which show that the Grey Reef Shark will attack if cornered, provoked or threatened. Its nature could be compared to that of a frisky dog with a bone.

Diving with Grey Reef Sharks

Grey Reef Sharks are very popular on shark dives. When divers enter the water, they often swim in rapidly, no doubt attracted by the commotion caused by noisy divers. They then usually swim away to patrol their reef. When accustomed to people in the water they will put on a dazzling display which may culminate in a feeding frenzy, all with minimum danger to the spectators.

FINELY TUNED SENSES

Tests with underwater speakers have shown that Grey Reef Sharks are attracted by low-frequency vibrations similar to those produced by a struggling fish.

While other sharks may display aggressive body language, none are more explicit than the Grey Reef Shark. Typical warning displays are an arched back, dropped pectoral fins and an exaggerated swaying swimming motion. If deliberately provoked the shark may then attack with lightning speed to deliver one or more bites before swimming away. While the bites are serious they are rarely fatal. People most often attacked are spearfishers or careless divers that corner an animal in a reef canyon.

Silvertip Shark

The streamlined Silvertip Shark is one of the most beautiful of all sharks. Silvertips are similar in appearance to Grey Reef Sharks, having a clean tapered body and typical shark contours, but their pectoral fins have bright silver tips, as does the trailing edge of the tail. The Grey Reef Shark has dark pectoral tips and rear tail edge. The Silvertip is grey with a bronzy

The silvertip scientific species name, 'albimarginatus', means 'white edges' and refers to its distinctive markings.

sheen becoming lighter as it blends into a pure white belly. The tips of the dorsal fins are always white; confusingly this is sometimes the case with the Grey Reef Shark, too.

Silvertips can become frisky when baited but, like all sharks, they prefer to keep some distance from swimmers. Females carry up to 11 young for 12 months before giving birth during the summer. The perfectly formed 55–80 cm pups grow to an adult size of 2 m, living on a diet of tropical fish, which they hunt among the reefs.

Galapagos Shark

This shark was first recorded in the Galapagos archipelago but has since been recorded in many oceanic islands of the Pacific. Its distribution is restricted in Australia to Lord Howe Island and surrounding oceanic reefs, being very plentiful at Middleton and Elizabeth Reefs. At first glance this shark is very

While similar to other whaler sharks, the Galapagos Shark is usually found only on offshore islands and reefs.

similar to the Grey Reef Shark with comparable markings, colour and profile but the Galapagos Shark has a far more slender body, especially when young, and a slightly rounded dorsal fin.

Female Galapagos Sharks are often seen with deep mating scars caused by males biting their gills, fins and flanks in a dominance display. Pups are born 60–80 cm long and grow to an adult size of 3 m. They feed primarily on fish and squid. Like the Grey Reef Shark, the Galapagos Shark also has a threat display that is used to warn off predators or competitors looking for food or territory.

How do we Learn about Sharks in the Wild?

Large mobile sharks that live in the open sea are very difficult to study by direct observation.

*M*uch can be learnt about animals by keeping them in captivity. However many shark species do not stay fit and healthy in aquariums due to their large size and their need for large territories. Tawny Nurse Sharks, however, have been studied in captivity as they are hardy bottom-dwelling sharks that neither migrate nor have large territories.

In the wild a tagging program has been used to good effect in tracking the movements of sharks. A shark tag is a sharp piece of barbed metal that has a number- or colour-coded string attached. A spear shaft that holds the tag is used to lodge the barb under the skin near the base of the dorsal fin. When the shark is recaptured the number or code is submitted to the relevant fishing authority who then adds the information to an ever-growing database. This information helps to track the seasonal movements and growth rates of various shark species.

Research in a Natural Environment

No method of research, however, is more valuable than studying the animals in their own environment. Of course, following a shark for a prolonged period of days, weeks or years, as is sometimes done with land animals, is impossible in an underwater environment. Observing mating, birth and courtship of sharks in the wild is very rare and feeding behaviour is usually restricted to artificial baiting. Field observations will progress according to the ingenuity of researchers, who may come up with new ways of utilising modern technology to follow and observe sharks in the wild.

Tags provide information on migration, distribution and growth rates when tagged sharks are recaptured.

Do Sharks Migrate?

*S*ome species of shark travel great distances while others spend their entire life in a confined territory. One Blue Shark was tagged in 1985 off the coast of the United States and was recaptured again near Africa, a distance of 6000 km. A Mako Shark tagged off northern New South Wales was recaptured off the coast of New Zealand after travelling over 2000 km.

The Port Jackson Shark has been reliably tracked over its extensive mating migration path.

Breeding seasons and water temperature govern many shark movements. Warm-water currents carry some sharks great distances as they follow their prey of schooling fish. Port Jackson Sharks have been known to travel up to 800 km to breed in early spring on the central New South Wales coast.

> **A TRACKING RECORD**
> The shark-tracking record must surely belong to two Sandbar Sharks tagged in the same week of 1965. Almost 20 years later they were recaptured 1600 km away from the original tagging site but a mere 160 km apart.

Are Sharks Loners?

*L*arge predatory sharks usually only come together to mate or when a large food source, such as a dead whale, is to be found. Some bottom-dwelling sharks may have a large area in common but do not school or socialise. However, there are still other sharks that often school or feed in loose aggregations.

School Sharks are found in groups of the same size and sex. Grey Nurse Sharks spend their daylight hours together in schools of 2–200 individuals, often packed together in sheltered caverns or gullies. Scalloped Hammerhead Sharks can gather in groups of several hundred during the day but they disperse at night to feed.

Scalloped Hammerheads are noted for their social behaviour, forming large schools where mating behaviour has been observed.

Tiger Shark

Tiger Sharks are common throughout their range, feeding on an impressive variety of prey and carrion.

From knee-deep shallow sandy lagoons to deep ocean walls, the Tiger Shark is the king of tropical sharks. A blunt, almost square snout, large black eyes rimmed with white and broad dark bands on the back and flanks easily distinguish this shark from any other. The teeth are a distinctive cockscomb shape, ideal for a wide variety of prey.

Born at 50 cm long, distinctly striped juveniles can grow to 6 m. Sharks over 3.5 m become very deep bodied and heavy. At maturity the broad dark bands may fade almost completely to an overall mid- to dark grey; on the flanks the fading colour merges with the white belly. Females give birth to litters of 10–80 pups 12 months after conception. Their lifespan is about 12–13 years.

WATER TIGERS

Tiger Sharks have attacked, killed and even eaten humans on occasion so they should be treated with the utmost respect. However when confronted with divers, they are usually very cautious and shy, coming in only briefly to satisfy their curiosity before departing for deep water.

Indiscriminate Feeders

Unlike many other sharks, the Tiger Shark has an indiscriminate appetite. Objects as bizarre and diverse as plastic toys and human remains have been found in their stomachs. At regular seasonal intervals, however, Tiger Sharks are known to feed on specific prey. For example, they appear to know the precise locations and times of the year that certain animals, such as turtles and birds, breed and they turn up on cue to feast on the old, young, sick or unwary.

Oceanic Whitetip Shark

Only the Oceanic Whitetip Shark has such distinctive, large rounded fins.

Even though the Oceanic Whitetip Shark is considered one of the five most dangerous sharks in the world, it is rarely, if ever, seen by swimmers and snorkelers. This shark is only found in offshore oceanic waters with temperatures of over 20°C.

Encounters are usually by anglers over the continental shelf while searching for game fish or by divers visiting outer reefs with deep reef walls. They are also often found with pods of Pilot Whales, following these socially active mammals in the hope of picking up scraps of squid or fish.

Oceanic Whitetip Sharks are very distinctive. Growing to 3.5 m long, they have a typical fusiform whaler profile but with very long paddle-shaped pectoral fins and a tall dorsal fin, all with broadly rounded tips marked by a blotch of cream or white. The white markings on the tips can also be found on the pelvic fins and both lobes of the tail. These white markings are usually black on young sharks up to a length of 1.3 m. Body colour ranges from a bronzy grey to a mottled khaki.

A Swift Hunter

Unlike sharks that live over densely populated reefs, the Oceanic Whitetip must cover a lot of territory to find its food. When food does become available there is no time for the shark to check for potential danger as the prey may just as easily be taken by other predators. For this reason the Oceanic Whitetip Shark charges in very quickly on any possible prey, a habit that makes it dangerous to divers or swimmers and it has been blamed for the deaths of many survivors of ship or plane disasters at sea.

Whitetip Reef Shark

At times the Whitetip Reef Shark has been seen in schooling aggregations where mating takes place.

Not to be confused with the Oceanic Whitetip, the Reef Whitetip Shark is probably the most common shark encountered by divers and snorkelers on tropical reefs. While it has the potential to give a serious bite if molested, it is generally considered to be harmless to humans.

This shark has a small, broad and flattened head. The protective ridges above its eyes give it the appearance of having a permanent scowl. A white tip is present on the first and sometimes on the second dorsal fin as well as the tail lobes. Its body is dark grey, sometimes with small, dark scattered spots, becoming lighter on the flanks to blend with a white belly.

HUNTING IN TIGHT SPACES

During the night the normally docile Whitetip Reef Sharks become very active, searching out fish, octopuses, cuttlefish, crabs and lobsters. Their tough hides, slender bodies, blunt snouts and protective eye ridges enable them to move and hunt in very confined spaces within the reef.

Mating Observations

During the day this shark can be found resting on the seabed, either in the open, under a ledge or in caves within a loose territorial area. The Whitetip Reef Shark is one of the few sharks seen while mating. The male lies alongside the female and grasps her pectoral fins firmly in his mouth. As the pair lie vertically in the water with their heads on the coral reef, he inserts one clasper into her genital opening. Tawny Nurse Sharks mate in a similar manner.

Blacktip Reef Shark

Australian Aborigines once prepared a meat dish, called buunhdaarr, from Blacktip Reef Sharks.

There are three species of blacktip shark in Australian waters; all look almost identical to the untrained eye. The Blacktip Reef Shark is a common species usually found in shallow inshore reefs and lagoons; the other two species are more oceanic in their range.

As its name suggests the Blacktip Reef Shark has black tips on all of its fins, with larger areas of black on the lower tail lobe and the first dorsal fin. The body colour can vary from grey to yellowish brown with a pearly blaze on the flanks.

Two to four young are born each November. They start life as perfectly formed 50 cm miniatures of their parents and grow to 1.8 m. Their broad diet includes reef fish, crabs, shells and squid. In northern Australia 25 per cent of stomach contents were found to be snakes.

Often Seen in the Shallows

This shark is usually seen by waders, snorkelers and divers in very shallow water. As the tide comes in over exposed coral reef platforms it follows the rising waters hunting and feeding as it goes. At times it is in water so shallow that the dorsal and tail fins are exposed like a frame out of a clichéd shark cartoon.

On rare occasions waders have been bitten by this species, an accident resulting from the shark mistaking a foot or leg for a struggling fish. Under normal circumstances the Blacktip Reef Shark is a curious but inoffensive animal, approaching divers and snorkelers before resuming its search of the reef.

Are Sharks Voracious Eating Machines?

Hungry Grey Reef Sharks may burst into a feeding frenzy when overwhelmed by a desire to eat.

Sharks certainly have been burdened with the reputation of just being a fearsome mouth with fins. However impartial research has shown that sharks do not need to feed every day and often go without food for many days or weeks. Since all shark species have a body temperature that is maintained at a rate close to the surrounding environment they do not need large quantities of food, as we do, to provide heat.

Pelagic or open-ocean sharks take full advantage of every feeding occasion as the next meal may be a long way off. For example a dead whale carcass will attract large numbers of sharks, which then feed until totally bloated. Often there are spectacular displays of feeding 'frenzies', thrashing about above and below the surface to take large chunks of flesh. What is not so well known is that those same sharks may not feed again for many days or even weeks.

INTERMITTENT MEALS
It has been estimated that a 30 kg meal taken by a Great White Shark will last it for 45 days and a Lemon Shark will eat 2–5 per cent of its body weight every 40–80 hours. In human terms that is approximately one burger and fries every two to three days.

When do Sharks Feed?

Given the opportunity a shark will feed at any time. However they are usually far more active at dawn and dusk with night-time being the favoured period for hunting. This is when many of the reef species, including fish, are asleep which makes them easier to hunt down and capture.

How do Sharks Store Energy?

Mammals store their main energy reserves as fat. Sharks do not possess a fat layer but instead store their excess calories as oil, called squalene, in their livers.

A shark's liver makes up approximately 25 per cent of its body weight. It has been estimated that a 9 m long Basking Shark weighing 6.5 tonnes would have a liver weighing 940 kg, producing a massive 2270 litres of oil. Besides storing

The trailing intestines of a recently consumed seal or dolphin will be stored by this Great White Shark as squalene oil.

energy, the liver also provides flotation for the shark as it does not possess a gas bladder like other fish. Squalene is 5–6 times more buoyant than water.

What do Sharks Eat?

There are two basic types of food that sharks eat: either free-swimming animals, such as fish and squid, or sedentary animals, such as molluscs and sea urchins. Bottom-dwelling sharks feed on animals found on the reef, such as crabs, shelled invertebrates, sea urchins and worms, while open-ocean or free-swimming sharks feed on fish and squid.

Of course there are cross-overs and exceptions to these general rules. Some bottom-dwelling sharks, such as wobbegongs, feed mostly on fish and Zebra Sharks will also eat small fish found on the reef. Tiger Sharks, which eat almost anything, have been found with large helmet shells, roughly the size of a human head, in their stomachs. Adult Great White Sharks, Makos and Seven Gill Sharks favour fish but they also feed on large marine mammals such as seals, whales and dolphins. Whale Sharks eat plankton. While many sharks do feed on carrion, fresh food is always preferred over rancid meat.

A Crested Horn Shark attempts to eat the egg of a Port Jackson Shark.

Hammerhead Sharks

The distinctive hammer-shaped head allows these shark species to exploit a wide variety of prey, both on the reef and in the open ocean.

There are four species of hammerhead shark found in Australian waters, ranging in size from 1.9 to 6 m. The Smooth Hammerhead, which at times forms large schools, is found only in southern waters, mostly in shallow bays and reefs down to depths of 20 m. Its head has a smooth, bow-like leading edge with no central indentation.

The similar Scalloped Hammerhead is found in tropical to warm temperate waters from the surface down to 300 m. The leading edge of the wing-like head has a central indentation and is flanked by two more scalloped indentations. The rather shy Scalloped Hammerhead is most famous for forming large schools during the daytime. It feeds on fish and squid at night in deep water.

The Winghead Shark is the smallest hammerhead, growing to only 1 m long. It is easily distinguished by the long rectangular wings on the head projecting well out from the body. It is found in the far north in shallow and often silty water.

A Dangerous Species

Unlike the other hammerhead species, which are considered harmless, the Great Hammerhead has the potential to be dangerous. It has an indentation in the centre of the head and a very tall, curved dorsal fin. It does not school like other species but single animals are found around offshore tropical reefs.

A USEFUL, IF CURIOUS, SHAPE

The amazing hammer-shaped head of the hammerhead sharks provides for a large sweep of its scent, sight and electro-sensory equipment. The winged shape of the head also allows the shark to manoeuvre very quickly as it twists and turns after speedy prey.

Bronze Whaler

The name bronze whaler is mistakenly used to identify many different species of tropical whaler sharks. In Australia the Bronze Whaler is a single species found only in cool southern waters, from Coffs Harbour, around the southern States, to Jurien Bay in Western Australia.

In profile, the Bronze Whaler has a distinctly pointed snout and its body has a bronzy sheen.

From a size of 60 cm at birth, adults grow to 3 m. The brown to grey body colour has an obvious bronze sheen. Many other species of sharks may also display a bronze glow, especially in bright sunlight. The flanks have a pale blaze from below the dorsal fin to the tail. The margins or tips of the fins may be dusky but they are never black or obviously patterned. The snout of the Bronze Whaler is distinctly pointed in profile, although this is less obvious from other angles.

Bronze Whalers are often seen close inshore feeding on schooling fish, such as salmon, frequently within the surf zone. They are also found around offshore islands over deep water where they prey on squid as well as pelagic and bottom-dwelling fish.

Blue Shark

This beautifully coloured shark is an open-ocean migrator. It has a long, slender body with a large eye and long snout. The pectoral fins are elongated, giving it an overall elegant appearance. Its back is a deep indigo blue fading down the flanks to a pure white belly. Females have skin three times thicker than males to protect them during boisterous mating behaviour.

Blue Sharks are easily identified by their colour, large eyes and slender proportions.

The Blue Shark has an international distribution greater than any other species. At one time it was the most common shark in the open oceans but overfishing has reduced its numbers considerably.

Squid make up a large portion of the Blue Shark's diet, along with schooling fish, such as anchovies and pilchards but they will also feed on carrion or fish caught on set long lines. Under normal circumstances they are inoffensive but their persistence can be unnerving and they should be treated with respect.

OTHER SHARKS

Sixgill Sharks

The Bluntnose Sixgill Shark likes cold water and so remains at depth in tropical areas.

There are three species of sixgill sharks in Australian waters. The Frilled Shark is found only in very deep water, although it will come near the surface on rare occasions. The Bigeye Sixgill and Bluntnose Sixgill Sharks may occur in shallow water, especially when they are juveniles but they are normally found at depths of 90–2000 m.

The Bluntnose Sixgill Shark has a wide tropical to temperate international distribution, being found locally in southeastern Australia, confined areas of Queensland and Western Australia. It has green-tinted eyes and a mouth that appears to be a tight-lipped grin. Its one dorsal fin is set well back on the body, near the elongated tail. The torso is round, almost chubby, and the six gill slits continue well around the throat.

The teeth of the lower jaw resemble a hand saw, with a series of jagged sloping points on a long base. The upper teeth have similar rear-pointing spikes but on a shorter base and with only three points, perfect for holding large or small prey. The whole array is ideal for slicing apart both large quarry, such as dolphins and sharks, as well as holding smaller animals like crabs and squid.

An Unknown Biology

Despite it being a well-known commercial species, very little is known of the Bluntnose Sixgill Shark's biology except that females do not reach breeding maturity until they are 4.5 m long. They then can carry enormous litters up to and exceeding 100 young. These begin life at 70 cm long but they grow to an enormous size: up to 5 m long in some cases.

Sevengill Sharks

The colour and gill count of the Broadnose Sevengill shark make it easy to identify in shallow southern seas.

There are two species of sevengill shark in Australia. The Sharpnose Sevengill Shark is a comparatively small animal, growing to 1.4 m. It is found mostly in deeper water down to 1000 m and is rarely encountered except by deep-sea fishermen. The Broadnose Sevengill Shark is found in shallow bays near the surface or over reefs down to 150 m. Females give birth to 40 cm long young which grow to 3 m.

Broadnose Sevengill Sharks have a short broad snout and head, small eyes and a mouth that appears to sport a gummy smile. They have a single dorsal fin set well back on the body near the elongated tail. Their body colour varies from brown to a silvery grey, with distinctive black and white spots scattered over the back and flanks. The bottom teeth are saw shaped with rear-pointing tips, while the upper teeth have two points or cusps that pierce and hold their prey.

MOSTLY INOFFENSIVE
In the wild this shark is curious and will approach divers, often being seen by abalone divers. It is considered inoffensive but with the potential to be dangerous. The only reported attacks have been on divers in aquariums.

Pack Hunting
The Broadnose Sevengill has been observed hunting in packs. As it grows larger it begins to actively hunt for bigger prey, including seals that live in its southern range. Seals are fast and wary in the water so pack hunting increases the chance of success with a kill feeding all that are involved. They also feed as individuals on fish and squid as well as carrion and other sharks.

What is a Lateral Line?

All sharks possess a lateral line but it is not always as apparent as it is on the Great White Shark.

The lateral line is literally a line that runs along the flanks of sharks. Beneath the surface, the line is made up of small canals filled with sensory cells that detect changes in water pressure. These cells are also found on the face and snout of sharks and enable them to sense movement in the water as well as solid objects.

In university experiments it was found that an effectively blind and deaf shark could still avoid solid objects, such as the walls of a tank, and that when the lateral system was blocked the shark lost that ability. The lateral line system helps sharks to sense prey, predators and the environment in limited visibility.

Can Sharks Smell?

Sharks have very sensitive nostrils capable of picking up odours in minute amounts. For example tests have shown that a starved shark can sense scent dilutions as great as 1 part per10 billion. This acute sense of smell is used by sharks to track down their prey from tiny traces of chemicals that animals release. It is also very useful in breeding when males can smell females from a distance or among a school of mixed sharks.

This Grey Spotted Catshark has especially large and elaborate nostrils.

How do Sharks find Hidden Prey?

A shark may be attracted by vibrations felt in the water via its lateral line or may track down its prey using vision and smell but when it comes to animals concealed by sand, silt or darkness the shark uses its sensitive electrical sensors.

On the snout, mouth and face small jelly-filled pits called 'ampullae of Lorenzini' pick up the infinitesimal electrical impulses generated by muscle tissue. The sensitivity of this system is calculated to be able to pick up .01 microvolts or 1/100 millionth of a volt per square centimetre 25 cm away from buried prey.

The small black dots on this Grey Nurse Shark's face are electro-receptors.

A Case of Mistaken Identity

A tiny electric current is formed from the galvanising effect of seawater upon metal. This can attract curious sharks that think they have found a tasty morsel. Sharks will often bump or bite metal objects, such as engine propellers, as they investigate what seems to be an electrical signal sent out by potential prey.

SHARKS WITH EARS
You may not have seen them but sharks do have 'ears'. Two small holes on top of the head are connected to inner ears that are used to pick up low vibrations and sound-pressure waves. Sharks are able to respond very quickly and accurately to vibrations in the water.

Can Sharks Taste their Food?

O n the insides of sharks' mouths are small lumps that are covered with tastebuds. After sight, sound, pressure sensitivity, touch, scent and electrical signals are detected and acted upon, as a final test the tastebuds tell the shark if the food it is eating is acceptable. Some fish and shells are able to expel chemical repellents to which sharks react. Of course it's always possible that the tastebuds are there to help them enjoy a fine meal as well, just as we do.

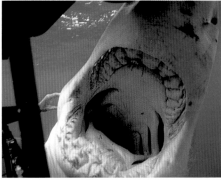
A Great White has tastebuds on the roof of its mouth.

Bramble Sharks

The deep-dwelling Bramble Shark has a rough exterior of enlarged denticles.

*T*here are two species of bramble sharks in the world: the Prickly Shark, which grows to 4 m, and the Bramble Shark, which grows to 2.6 m. Both are found in cool southern waters off South Australia and Victoria in depths of 70–900 m. They are almost identical in appearance, having stout rounded bodies, small slightly flattened heads, and two small dorsal fins set so well back that they are next to the broad elongated caudal or tail fins. There are pelvic fins, no anal fins, five pairs of gills and a set of small spiracles.

The colouring of the two species differs slightly, with Prickly Sharks being greyish brown all over with black edges to their fins and pale or white under the snout and around the mouth. The Bramble Shark has a grey to brown body colour, sometimes with a purplish tinge, but with a paler belly. It may have small dark spots on the back and flanks.

A Raspy Skin and a Throat that Vacuums

The hide of most sharks have a rough covering of small tooth-like scales called denticles that give them a characteristic raspy coat. Normally denticles are very small and best seen with a magnifying glass but those of the Bramble Shark are prominent — as large as 1.5 cm across the base — and scattered all over the body in small clusters. The Prickly Shark also has denticles but they are smaller, only 0.5 cm across the base, and they do not form clusters.

The teeth in both species are blade-like, ideal for holding and slicing. It is thought that they vacuum up prey, rapidly opening their mouth and throat to suck in small sharks, squid, crabs and fish.

Dogfish

Some dogfish, such as this Golden Dogfish, are found only in deep water.

*D*ogfish are the largest shark family in Australia with 40 species. They range from the smallest of all sharks, the Smalleye Pygmy Shark, at 22 cm long, to the huge 6 m long Pacific Sleeper Shark. All dogfish have large spiracles, two dorsal fins, often with a sharp defensive spine, and lack an anal fin.

Most species are deep-water dwellers, inhabiting the 100–2000 m depth range, but some, like the White-Spotted Spurdog that lives on the southern coast, can be found in shallow bays. It would be unusual for any diver or snorkeler to see a dogfish but anglers find them regularly and some species are an important component of the commercial catch.

Taking a Cut

The 50 cm-long Cookie Cutter Shark is a notorious hit-and-run merchant. During the night it migrates from the depths to the surface and latches itself onto any large animal, such as a tuna, dolphin or whale. It then removes a plug of flesh from its victim before racing away. The lips act as a suction cup to hold it onto the side of its host, while the pointed upper teeth grasp the flesh. The lower teeth are blade-like and slice out a circular chunk of meat as the shark spins on its axis.

FISH THAT LIGHT UP

Lantern sharks are a group of dogfish that glow in the dark. Their bellies, flanks and tails have luminescent organs that may attract prey or help hide them from the predators beneath as the glow blends in with the faint star- or moonlight at the surface.

Do Sharks have Good Eyesight?

The eye of this Port Jackson Shark has a tightly constricted pupil in bright light.

Sharks have eyes with a similar construction to our own but they also have excellent vision underwater. They have a retina that gathers light with both rod and cone cells. The cone cells are used in bright light and are also sensitive to colour. In the past it was assumed that sharks were colour blind but experiments have shown that at least some sharks are able to distinguish between colours and colour patterns. The rod cells perceive contrast and are used for night vision to accentuate shape or differentiate between objects. Sharks have far more rods than cones, which makes their eyesight well matched to their habit of feeding at dusk, dawn or during the night.

Low-light Vision
Behind a shark's retina is a layer of silvery plates. These plates give the retina a second dose of light by acting like mirrors that reflect light back into the retina. This function allows the shark's eyes to perform far more efficiently that ours do in low light. Sharks that swim at the surface during the day or which inhabit sandy shallow water with very bright reflections are able to cover these plates with membranes made of dark pigment cells to effectively turn off this function.

Are all Sharks' Eyes the Same?

The proportionally large eyes of catsharks enable these nocturnal hunters to see better at night.

A shark's iris varies in shape depending on the species; sometimes it is a slit or circle that responds rapidly to changes in light levels. Bottom-dwelling sharks that live in shallow water tend to have small eyes as they find their prey by scent and electro-reception but open-water or deep-water sharks tend to have large eyes to take full advantage of any available light to catch fast-moving prey.

What Colour are Sharks' Eyes?

*T*he common per-
ception is that
sharks only have
cold black eyes. True,
some sharks such as
the Great White
Shark or thresher
sharks have plain
black eyes but many
others have an iris
that is silver, gold
or even patterned to
match their camou-
flage. Many deep-
water species have
beautiful green eyes.

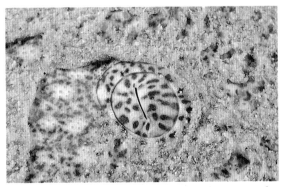

The colour of both the iris and the internal eye of different species of sharks can vary quite considerably. This is an angelshark's eye.

Do Sharks have Eyelids?

*H*umans need
to blink to moist-
en and clean the
surface of the eye but
sharks live in a liquid
environment where
there is no need for
this function. In fact,
sharks do have eye-
lids but in most
species they are
fixed so they cannot
close their eyes. The
Draughtboard Shark
and Blind Shark are
exceptions.

In addition, many
species of sharks have

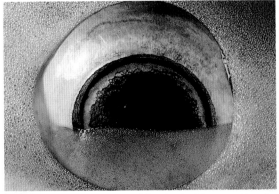

The partly deployed nictitating eyelid on this shark is operated by a small muscle next to the eye.

another eyelid called a nictitating eyelid. This eyelid is a tough transparent
membrane that is pulled across the eye by a specialised muscle. When any
object comes too close, the muscle contracts activating the membrane; the
response is similar to our blinking. This eyelid reflex is most often seen when
sharks are feeding. Those sharks without nictitating eyelids are able to roll the
eye up into the skull out of harm's way.

Angel Sharks

Like all angel sharks, the Australian Angel Shark is an efficient ambush hunter.

*T*he flattened appearance of an angel shark is very similar to that of a ray. Angel sharks have two dorsal fins well back on the body near the tail, which has symmetrical lobes. The large pelvic fins protrude from the body so that they match the contours of the broad pectoral fins. The head and body are flattened, with the skull between the eyes being concave or convex depending on the species.

There are 14 species of angel sharks, four of which are found in Australia. These range in size from 60 cm to 1.6 m. Found on all coasts except the far north to a depth of 400 m, angel sharks are bottom-dwellers that feed mainly on fish and squid but they also eat cuttlefish, crabs and occasionally shelled invertebrates. The angel sharks have a denser mass compared to other sharks, enabling them to lie still on the bottom.

ANGELS OF STEALTH

All angel sharks capture their prey by ambush. Lying almost invisible beneath a layer of sand they wait until a hapless victim approaches too close before engulfing it with lightning speed. Their narrow pointed teeth are ideal for holding prey, most of which is swallowed whole. Tests on the feeding habits of angel sharks have shown that they react to any passing prey, spitting out anything that does not appeal to the appetite. They have complete faith in their camouflage when approached by divers but will inflict a shallow bite if harassed.

Australian Angels

Four species of angel sharks are endemic to Australia. The most common, the Australian Angel Shark, is the largest, growing to 1.6 m or more. It is the only species found in shallow water from 2–150 m down. Between 10 and 20 young are born as living, hunting minia-tures of their parents. They have a unique spotted pattern on their lower caudal fin and distinctive white edges to the pectoral fins.

Sawsharks

Barbels and side gills (above) and teeth extending onto the head (inset) identify sawsharks.

The most obvious feature of the sawsharks are their elongated blade-like snouts studded with teeth of various sizes. These unusual creatures, ranging from 80 cm to 1.4 m, are rarely seen by divers but they are sometimes caught in gill nets set off beaches and taken seasonally by commercial trawlers. They are sold as 'Red Dog' in some areas or they become part of that vaguely described product known as flake.

Ranging from the shallows of the southern coast to 300–400 m deep on the continental shelf off Queensland, there are four species of sawshark in Australian waters. The Southern Sawshark enters shallow bays and estuaries in Tasmania and inhabits the southern coast, from the Victorian to the Western Australian border.

Unique Features

Sawsharks are easily confused with sawfish, which also have an elongated snout with teeth-like spikes and a similar body shape. There are two obvious differences: first are the tendrils on the snout of sawsharks which are missing on sawfish; second, sawsharks have gills on the sides of their heads like most sharks, while the sawfish, being types of rays, have their gills underneath their heads.

The sawsharks' tendrils, which are found about halfway along the length of their snout or 'saw', are used to sense hidden prey in sandy or silty areas while the toothed saw is used to slash at passing fish. To prevent damage to the mother, sawsharks have their replaceable saw teeth folded back until they are born.

Are Sharks Endangered?

Some species of shark have become rare or no longer commercially viable due to overfishing of either the shark or its prey. Whiskery Sharks in Western Australia and Gummy Sharks on the southern coast of Australia are now overfished. Blue and Oceanic Whitetip Sharks were once very common in the open ocean but driftnet and line fishing has severely reduced their numbers. Sharks are particularly vulnerable to any exploitation as they have long lifespans coupled with slow growth rates. Some sharks produce as few as one or two young each year or may only breed every two or three years.

Overfishing has heavily reduced the numbers of Oceanic Whitetips and other shark species.

Are Sharks Protected?

Contrary to much media hype, the Grey Nurse Shark has a docile nature and was the first shark to receive some legal protection.

The Grey Nurse Shark, which received protection in New South Wales in 1984, was the first shark ever to be protected anywhere in the world. Prior to this, sensationalist media and public opinion had pointed the blame for some shark attacks on the Grey Nurse Shark, which unfortunately had a gaping toothy grin that suited the unfounded rumours.

Anglers and divers used hooks, spearguns and deadly powerheads loaded with shotgun and rifle cartridges to kill off entire populations of Grey Nurse Sharks. When numbers plummeted and the sharks were found to be no threat to swimmers, action was taken to protect the species from further decline.

The Great White Shark is also protected. Trophy hunters have had some impact on their numbers but many more Great White Sharks are drowned in commercial fishing nets and their food staple of Southern Bluefin Tuna has been fished almost beyond commercial viability.

What Sharks do People Eat?

*H*uge fishing fleets around the world target sharks for their meat, oil, hides and fins. Various species of dogfish, such as the Endeavour Dogfish, and hound sharks, such as Whiskery, School and Gummy Sharks, make up most of the commercial catch. The bottom-dwelling wobbegongs and angel sharks are caught on drop lines or by trawlers, and end up in fish shops around Australia, usually sold under the generic name of flake.

School Sharks, like many other species of sharks, are destined for the dinner table, usually sold as 'flake'.

Sharks are an especially common food source in developing countries where indigenous people have long exploited them for food. Some native Australian tribes have traditionally caught small shallow-water sharks at certain times of the year when these sharks gathered for feeding or breeding purposes.

What Products are Made from Sharks?

*M*ost people have eaten shark meat but there are many other products that come from sharks. Shark-fin cartilage is the basis for many Asian dishes, such as soups and dumplings, as well as traditional Chinese medicine. Squalene oil, found in shark liver, is an extremely rich source of Vitamin A and is used in the pharmaceutical and cosmetics industries.

Ornaments and jewellery, as well as decorative or functional cutting implements, are made from shark teeth. In western medicine, cartilage has been turned into tablet form as an unproven method of controlling growths and cancers. The raspy hide of many sharks is used as sandpaper or as a non-slip gripping surface, such as for sword and knife handles. The hide is also made into leather for use as practical or decorative articles such as bags, book binding or shoes. Perhaps most startling is the use of shark corneas as a substitute in human cornea transplants.

Exotic dishes, medicines, dietary supplements and cosmetics may all contain shark products.

RAYS

What is a Ray?

The flattened, more rounded body shape of most rays make them easy to distinguish from the majority of sharks.

Of the 600 species of rays in the world, about 120 can be found in Australian waters. Like sharks, rays have a skeleton made of cartilage instead of bone. They also have denticles instead of flattened scales and the males have external claspers for reproduction. Like sharks, too, their upper jaws are not fused to their skulls.

Rays differ from sharks in having their pectoral fins attached to their heads, often forming a large disc. Also rays have no anal fins and their 5–6 pairs of gills are not on the sides of their heads but underneath.

Where are Rays Found?

*M*ost rays have flattened bodies that suit life on the seabed. However some species of ray are pelagic, that is they live above the bottom in open water. As far as depth is concerned, they can be found in water just a few inches deep or dredged up from the abyssal plain 1500–2000 m down or even more. Some species live in estuaries and one species, the Freshwater Whipray, is found in rivers far from the sea.

Rays prefer sandy or silty environments in which they can forage for prey and hide from passing predators.

Stingray or Stingaree?

*O*ften any flattened, bottom-dwelling ray is referred to as a stingray but stingrays and stingarees are two distinctly separate families of rays that commonly occur at all water depths.

Stingrays are large animals with adult wingspans of usually over 30 cm wide and commonly reaching 2 m or more. The tail is long and narrow, sometimes whip-like, and terminates in a pointed tip (unless damaged).

The rounded caudal fin at the tip of the tail identifies this ray as a stingaree.

Stingarees are much smaller, usually less than 50 cm wide. The tail is comparatively short, thick or more fleshy and it always has a rounded tip or caudal fin.

Do Stingrays really Sting?

*M*any ray families have barbed spines on the tail that are used for defence. When provoked a ray can swipe its tail with power and accuracy to impale its spine into an attacker. The spine has jagged serrations that can tear at the wound or cause the brittle 'sting' to break off while embedded. The spine has two narrow grooves that carry venom along its length and a very thin skin coat which, when broken, releases the venom. The venom is not deadly but delivers severe pain.

> **GIANT RAY**
> The largest ray is the Manta Ray, which can grow up to 9 m across the 'wings' and weigh well over a tonne. Most Manta Rays, however, are 4–6 m wide, which is still a respectable size.

Harmless, but Accidents do Happen

People are rarely killed by rays, usually when a large animal has speared a major artery. Some rays show that they feel threatened or provoked by raising the tail or swimming with jerky movements. Most ray stings, however, come without warning when people stand or lean on a ray hidden under the sand. Waders should shuffle their feet when walking on sand to allow the ray to flee before contact is made. Rays are usually shy but may be curious about divers, even seeking out their company when trained with food. If treated with care, they are harmless to humans.

A ray's spine is used only for defence.

Sawfish

This Freshwater Sawfish is able to live in both saline and freshwater environments.

The sawfish family has five members in Australian waters, all found in northern tropical areas in salt- or freshwater environments. All have a distinctive elongated snout that has an almost constant width right up to the rounded tip and a row of similar-sized 'teeth' along each edge.

The smallest species, the Dwarf Sawfish, grows to 1.5 m or more, which is about the size of the largest sawshark. The Wide Sawfish is reputed to grow to 7.6 m, one of the biggest fish in the sea, but most sawfish would be found in the 2–5 m range with the young beginning life at about 50–60 cm long, including their 'saw'.

A LETHAL WEAPON

The long 'saw', studded with teeth, is a formidable weapon used in hunting and defence. The saw is used to slash at prey or to uproot bottom-dwelling fish and it can be a danger to humans that startle or capture a large specimen. Like the embryonic sawshark, a young sawfish prior to birth has this formidable weapon sheathed in a protective membrane and the usually rigid saw is soft and pliable.

Habitat

Four of the five species — the Green, Wide, Dwarf and Narrow Sawfish — occur in shallow coastal areas where they are usually caught in gill nets or offshore by prawn trawlers. The Freshwater Sawfish has only been reliably recorded from the upper reaches of estuaries, freshwater rivers and waterholes. At times it has been found up to 100 km from the coast or in waterholes that have been isolated from rivers for a number of years due to low annual floods.

Sharkfin Guitarfish

The White-spotted Guitarfish (above) can be easily confused with a shark due to its large dorsal fins and caudal fin, as can its close relative, the Shark Ray (inset).

Sharkfin guitarfish are rays with two tall dorsal fins and a large scythe-like tail. Swimmers and divers often mistake them for sharks due to their fins, swimming motion and large size. There are two sharkfin guitarfish in Australian waters; both feed on crabs and shelled invertebrates.

The White-spotted Guitarfish is often found resting on the seabed during the day, propped up on its pectoral fins as it slowly pumps water over its gills. It can grow 3 m long and to a weight of well over 200 kg. Despite its large size, this harmless animal can be safely and closely approached by divers and snorkelers.

Distribution and Descriptions

The White-spotted Guitarfish is common in the tropical north but sightings have been made of large adults in southern waters, too. The young are pale grey to yellow-brown in colour, with distinctive white spots along the sides to as far back as the first dorsal fin. They also have a large dark spot just above the pectoral fins that becomes indistinct or disappears at maturity. Large adults become a darker grey or almost black with fewer spots.

The less common Shark Ray or Bowmouth Guitarfish, which also lives in tropical waters, has a unique curved snout, a flattened head rising to a high-arched back studded with blunt thorns and two tall dorsal fins. Its colour varies from brown to grey, often with a beautiful bluish hue, and light spots are scattered over its body from behind the head, covering all dorsal and tail surfaces.

Shovelnose Rays

The Eastern Fiddler Ray (above) and the Eastern Shovelnose Ray (inset) both sport the typical translucent snout of shovelnose rays.

Shovelnose rays enjoy Australia-wide distribution. All are harmless and may be approached by snorkelers and divers. They can be divided into two distinct groups: the shovelnose rays and the fiddler or banjo rays.

Of the shovelnose rays, there are five species. These have pelvic fins joined to the body immediately behind the pectoral fins. They also have translucent pointed snouts, small rear-set dorsal fins and tails with a nearly straight, as opposed to a curved, rear edge. The shovelnose rays are often seen by snorkelers resting on the bottom during the day, usually on sand or seagrass beds where they feed on shells, crabs and worms.

Fiddler or Banjo Rays

The two species of fiddler rays also have translucent snouts but they are shorter and more rounded. The Eastern Fiddler Ray, found on the east coast from southern Queensland to the eastern Victorian border, has a brown body colour with shades of yellow or olive. It has a pattern of pale lilac bands edged with dark brown and a distinctive triangle between and behind the eyes. The Southern Fiddler Ray is found from the eastern Victoria border to Perth. It has a darker yellowish brown body colour decorated with blue-grey bands but these do not form a triangle between the eyes.

Both species can be found on reef, sand or seagrass beds where they feed on shelled invertebrates, crabs and worms, which they crush between their jaws.

Electric Rays

Body shape differentiates the Numbfish (above) from the Tasmanian Numbfish (inset). Both deliver a powerful electric shock.

*T*wo species of electric rays are found in shallow water and four other species that are usually picked up by trawlers live in deeper waters. As the name suggests, all have one asset in common: the ability to deliver an electric shock, which may be anything from a mild tingle to a body-contorting blow.

The Shocking Numbfish

The Numbfish, also known as the Coffin Ray (a name not due to any deadly attributes but to the shape of specimens that have been dried out in the sun), can be found in shallow water down to below 200 m. Their brown colouring can vary from pale pink to chocolate, sometimes with a blotchy or sandy pattern.

Numbfish are usually found buried in sand or silt waiting for their prey to swim within striking distance. When a crab or fish comes too close it is hit with an electric charge that stuns it so that the ray can feed without fear of retaliation or injury. This animal is capable of delivering a severe electric shock, as many divers and anglers have found, and it should be left alone.

> **AN INTRIGUING WRIGGLER**
> Numbfish are found camouflaged beneath a layer of sand with just their eyes and spiracles protruding. To tempt prey to within striking range some Numbfish have a small black worm that lives on the eye or spiracle. Its colour is in stark contrast to the sand and it performs a constant swaying dance which attracts fish to the ray. This is a commensal, not a parasitic, relationship as both the ray and worm benefit.

What do Rays Eat?

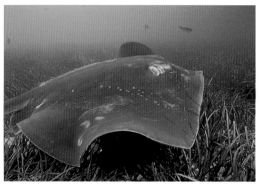

This Smooth Stingray has a widely varied diet, which includes fish and crabs. Most rays eat creatures that live on the seafloor.

Rays have strong crushing plates they use to mash their food. These plates, which line their powerful jaws, can grind tough shells or bones. Any pointed teeth that they may possess are used to hold or pull food into the mouth. Sawfish have additional teeth along their blade-like snout for this purpose.

Almost all rays eat animals that live on or below the seabed. Out of this seabed they dig or suck out shelled invertebrates, crabs or worms. All will eat fish if they can get them; some species, such as the numbfish, in fact have a high fish content in their diet. Others, such as the devilrays, feed on small fish and plankton, sifting out their food from the water without the need for any teeth.

How Do Rays Find Food?

This Black Stingray has an array of senses other than sight with which to detect food.

Since most of a ray's prey dwells in or on the seabed and rays' eyes are on top of their heads — usually elevated to allow the ray to search the surrounding area for potential predators — they cannot find their prey by sight. They have therefore developed remarkable senses of taste, touch, smell and electrical reception as their primary means of finding food.

Like sharks, rays have a very sensitive array of electro-receptors that they use to find prey. These detect minute electric currents generated by muscle tissue. The entire underside of a ray's disc — which is typically large — is sensitive to texture and vibration, so when the ray is actively hunting it covers a considerable area of the seabed. The nostrils are large and well developed for sensing any chemicals in the water that may indicate prey.

What Enemies Do Rays Have?

*M*any shark species prey on rays. Tiger and hammerhead sharks are often found with ray spines embedded in their jaws. One hammerhead shark was seen beating a ray into submission with its head before feeding. Killer Whales have also been photographed feeding on rays.

Like sharks, rays have urea in their blood to combat the high salt content in their cells. If the flesh is to be eaten by humans, it needs to be soaked in fresh water to eliminate the resulting ammonia scent. This process, along with a tendency for rays to be tough, makes them too bothersome for most consumers.

Tiger Sharks are among the many species of sharks that eat rays.

Can Rays Swim Backwards?

*B*ottom-dwelling rays swim by undulating their pectoral fins in a series of wave-like motions. By simply changing the action, a ray can swim in reverse or it can spin on its axis by reversing one fin. This ability gives the ray a high degree of manoeuvrability in its daily foraging activities; it is also useful if being attacked.

The wave-like motions of this stingaree's wings can be altered to enable it to reverse.

SOFT DELIVERIES DESPITE SPINES

When giving birth, female rays are protected from the spines of their pups by delivering them with their weapons soft and pliable. Rays that have large body 'thorns' are born with smooth skin and sawfish that have a tooth-studded snout come with a protective sheath that covers the soft flexible teeth.

Do Rays Lay Eggs?

*O*nly skates lay eggs. All other species of ray give birth to live young. Skates' eggs are rectangular and have tendrils that attach to growths on the seabed. Some egg cases also have a sticky coating that collects debris providing them with camouflage and adding extra weight for anchorage.

Smooth Stingray

Tail shape and small speckles on the disc are the main features that identify the Smooth Stingray.

The largest of the world's stingrays is the Smooth Stingray. It can weigh well over 350 kg, measure over 2 m across the wings and have an overall length of 4.5 m. At birth, they are 36 cm across the disc. It is common throughout its range, from southern Queensland around the south coast to Shark Bay in Western Australia.

The Smooth Stingray is dark grey to black above with a distinctive pattern of small white spots scattered across the base of the fins below and behind the eyes. The tail is thick with a single row of blunt thorns ending with one or two barbed spines midway along the tail, which then quickly tapers to a point. Anglers and commercial trawlers often catch this large ray and cut off the tail to prevent injury to themselves before throwing the ray back resulting in many of these rays getting by with amputated tails.

When Smooth Rays are Encountered

During summer months the Smooth Stingray can be found in water as shallow as 1 m or less, especially where fish are being cleaned, for example near boat ramps or piers. It has also been taken by trawlers and drop-line fisheries in water as deep as 500 m. The Smooth Stingray is curious and will approach swimmers and divers, especially if there is bait or berley in the water. While these animals are easily trained to take hand-held bait, they are potentially dangerous if they retain their large barbed spines. When threatened, cornered or molested they will curl their tails up and over their backs in a threat display.

UNRELIABLE TAILS
The tips of the long thin tails of stingrays, whiprays, eagle rays and devilrays are fragile and often damaged. Therefore with these animals, body size is normally measured across the wingtips.

Cowtail Stingray

Cowtail Stingrays are large rays found in tropical waters across the north of Australia. They grow to a maximum size of nearly 2 m and are common on reefs, usually seen resting in caves or deep ledges on sand. They are a uniform dark grey to black with a very long tapering tail, the underside of which has a a long narrow flap or 'banner' of skin that starts beneath the single barbed spine and ends

These Cowtail Stingrays, with their distinctive tail flaps, are involved in courting behaviour.

before the whip-like tip, which is sometimes missing on older animals.

While it may enter fresh water at times, the Cowtail Stingray is usually found in sandy areas around coral reefs where it forages for crabs, small fish, worms and shelled invertebrates which it crushes in its plate-like teeth. It will usually sit quietly when approached by divers or may even swim in for a close look. Although it is considered harmless, care should be taken of its large barbed spine.

Black Stingray

Found across southern coastal waters, the Black Stingray shares a similar habitat and appearance to the Smooth Stingray. It differs in having thorns along the middle of the back as well as at the base of the tail and the longer whip-like tail section beyond the spine is covered in small rough thorns that give it a spiky appearance. The armed tail, with its rough surface and large serrated spine, is a superb defence. Body colour is blue-grey to black.

While it does not grow as large as the Smooth Stingray, it can still attain a substantial weight of over 200 kg and a width of 1.8 m. Found as individuals or as large schools, they often gather for mating purposes. Black Stingrays feed on fish, crabs and shelled invertebrates which they search out in the sand using the sensitive electro-receptors located on their undersides. These rays are often used in large aquarium displays due to their impressive size and hardy nature.

The Black Stingray has a tail studded with small thorns.

Leopard Whipray

Few rays sport such a striking pattern as the Leopard Whipray. The entire upper surface, including half of the tail, is covered in a pattern of circular brown to black rings, just like a leopard. When undamaged, the tail is three times as long as the body and tapers to a fine point, like a whip, giving an elegant bearing to this beautiful ray.

The Leopard Whipray has quite a distinctive pattern. It has the long thin tail found on all whiprays.

The young are born at 20 cm wide and grow to at least 1.4 m across their wings. Leopard Whiprays are found in tropical waters from Shark Bay in Western Australia to at least the Queensland–New South Wales border; here they inhabit sandy seabeds in the open or near reefs and they feed on crabs, shrimp and shelled invertebrates. When resting they will cover themselves in sand for extra camouflage. Like most rays, they are considered to be harmless but because they are large and have serrated spines, they deserve respect.

Blotched Fantail Ray

The common name for the Blotched Fantail Ray comes from its coloration and tail flap. The upper surface is a pattern of black, grey and white spots and blotches that ends abruptly at the edges of the circular-shaped body. The pattern continues along the tail to the one or two spines where the colour changes to black or dark grey. The very edges of the body disc are white, like the belly. A flap of skin runs

This juvenile Blotched Fantail Ray clearly shows the white edge and blotched body pattern of its species.

along the underside of the tail, from the spine to the pointed tip.

This ray has a broad international distribution but in Australia it lives throughout the coastal waters of the northern tropics. It is common on coral reefs where it feeds on bottom-dwelling animals. While the Blotched Fantail Ray is approachable and at times curious, it should be treated with respect; at least one human fatality has been attributed to this ray.

Blue-spotted Maskray

Maskrays are a small group of stingrays with a band of dark colour across their eyes. The Blue-spotted Maskray usually has this dark eye-band sprinkled with a pattern of small dark spots. The body is brown to bluish grey with a scattered pattern of large blue spots edged with still darker blue. The end of the tail has a distinctive black and white banded pattern.

Blue-spotted Maskrays are often found in the daytime foraging across sand flats in tropical waters.

The Blue-spotted Maskray is common on tropical reefs across the north of Australia and throughout Asia. It can be found on shallow reef tops down to depths of 90 m. It is quite active during the day and can be closely approached, especially where snorkelers and divers regularly frequent the reefs. These rays forage over the reef and sand flats for hermit crabs, worms, shrimp and small fish. The young are born at 16 cm wide and grow to a wingspan of 40 cm.

Blue-spotted Fantail Ray

Normally hidden under ledges, the Blue Spotted Fantail Ray sports a pattern of vivid fluorescent blue spots.

No confusion should exist between the Blue-spotted Fantail Ray and the Blue-spotted Maskray as they are very different in appearance. The Blue-spotted Fantail Ray has a more rounded, egg-shaped disc with a very distinctive pattern of even-toned bright blue, almost florescent, spots over a mustard or yellow-brown body colour. It also lacks the dark mask.

The Blue-spotted Fantail Ray is very common on tropical reefs but it is flighty and difficult to approach during the day. Usually the only sign of this ray is the tail, normally with two spines, protruding from a sandy ledge. The eyes, raised well above the body, give it excellent panoramic vision and the very large spiracles, which channel clean water to the gills, allow it to feed freely on shelled invertebrates buried in the sand. The spines near the tip of its highly manoeuvrable tail can strike anywhere on or beyond its disc providing an excellent defence.

What is a Skate?

Although similar to the stingrays and sting-arees, the skates belong to a separate family. Unlike other rays, all but three species of Australian skates have two dorsal fins near the tip of the tail without an obvious caudal fin. The pelvic fins at the base of the tail are divided into two lobes. Skates do not possess a 'sting' or spine but they do possess varying amounts of sharp thorns on the tail, back, head and wings. Most skates also have a pointed nose that may be semi-transparent and is supported by an internal cartilage.

Can Eagle Rays Fly?

With their wide pointed fins beating through the water, the eagle rays certainly do look as if they are flying. At times they will also jump well above the surface but of course they are too heavy to actually fly in our atmosphere.

Eagle rays feed on shelled invertebrates which they find in sandy areas; their crushing plates are capable of mashing very large shells. While they feed on the bottom, they are most usually seen when swimming in open water near the surface, in groups of up to 20 or more.

White-spotted Eagle Rays flap their wings like birds, soaring in the open water column.

Which is the Most Common Eagle Ray?

*T*he most common species seen in tropical waters is the White-spotted Eagle Ray. The head, with a short pointed snout, projects well out from the body and the whip-like tail, when undamaged, can be 5–6 m long. A single spine at the base of the tail is used for defence when attacked from behind. The upper surface of the body is covered in a striking pattern of small white spots.

The raised and rounded head of this Southern Eagle Ray is typical of eagle rays.

In temperate waters the Southern Eagle Ray that feeds on crabs and shelled invertebrates in shallow water is the most commonly seen species. It has a raised head, with distinctive blue patches over a grey- to mustard-coloured back and grows to 1.3 m wide.

Are Devilrays Evil?

*D*evilrays are huge rays that feed on small fish and plankton. Only one of the four species found in Australian waters has a small stinging spine and the teeth in all species are minuscule. None is considered dangerous and at times these gentle giants seem to seek out the company of humans. So why are they called devilrays?

Back when the Earth was thought by some to be full of monsters, fishermen may have become frightened when devilrays leapt above the surface of the sea. On some occasions a devilray may have been caught on a line resulting in a wild ride as the powerful ray fled in fear. The two lobes at the front of the head may have been reminiscent of the devil's horns as depicted by the Italian poet, Dante, in his description of hell, and in such a way the common name stuck, much maligning the gentle character of this animal for ever more.

The Manta Ray, one of the devilrays, is a gentle acrobatic plankton feeder.

Crossback Stingaree

Also known as the Banded Stingaree, the Crossback Stingaree takes both its common and scientific names from the cross-shaped pattern of black markings on its back. This stingaree's body colour varies from pale brown or grey to golden yellow; the bands on the back are dark brown to black. The short, stout tail has one serrated spine that can be manoeu-

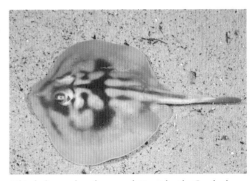

This dark cross-shaped pattern distinguishes the Crossback Stingaree from all other rays.

vred to defend any part of its body from attack by delivering a painful wound.

Waders and swimmers should be careful of this ray as it is usually well hidden under a covering of sand in shallow water. It can also be found on reefs and sand down to depths of 160 m throughout its Victorian and Tasmanian range. Not only are Crossback Stingarees found as isolated individuals; they also occur in small to large groups and often they mix with other species of stingarees. Females produce brightly marked pups in litters of 2–4 young that grow to an adult size of 50 cm long.

Eastern Shovelnose Stingaree

The Eastern Shovelnose Stingaree is similar to its western relative except that it is found only in the east.

The Eastern Shovelnose Stingaree is found near reefs along the coast of Victoria. The almost-identical Western Shovelnose Stingaree has a range that joins that of the Eastern Shovelnose Stingaree's and extends as far west as to Perth. The eastern species is found either in the open water or resting on the sandy floor of caves and ledges. It has a light to dark brown back with dark markings on the tail and sometimes in the middle of the back. A variable pattern of small dark to light brown or yellowish spots are scattered across its body. It is a large stingaree, growing to 80 cm long or more.

This ray is often found in shallow water, excavating a hollow as it forages after worms, crabs and burrowing fish. It is quite approachable and will carry on its daily activities if not harassed. Males can be distinguished by their large claspers with pear-shaped tips.

Sparsely-spotted Stingaree

This widespread stingaree has a variable body colour from light to mid-grey or pale brown. A pale U-shaped line joins the eyes and similar hazy lines occur on the wings. Sometimes this stingaree bears small dark spots and often, but not always, there are 2–10 white spots with dark edges of variable size on the wings near its raised body. These normally distinct dark-bordered white spots are often missing from

The Sparsely-spotted Stingaree is possibly the most common shallow-water stingaree around the Australian coast.

northern specimens, leading to confusion with other ray species but careful examination should reveal this stingaree's identity.

Sparsely-spotted Stingarees are born at about 12 cm long in small litters and grow to 40 cm. They are very common throughout their range, from northern New South Wales around the south coast to Perth, occurring from wading shallows down to depths of 150 m. They have a reputation for being aggressive toward swimmers and divers but if left undisturbed they are content to stay hidden in the sand.

Common Stingaree

True to its name, the Common Stingaree is easily found throughout its range from southern Queensland to the Victorian border. Its pale to dark brown, grey or even char-coal coloured body is without any consistent distinguishing patterns. It has one or two spines preceded by a small dorsal fin that may be reduced to a small fold of skin on some individuals. The rounded tail fin is black on juveniles, becoming paler in adults.

The Common Stingaree can have a variety of colours but it is usually dark grey to black like this large individual.

While the Common Stingaree can be found in water over 100 m deep, it is more usual at depths of less than 60 m and is often seen by snorkelers and divers in the shallows. It feeds on small shelled invertebrates, worms and crabs, and like most other rays, mating occurs with the male inserting one of its two claspers into the female as it curls its tail under and around her body.

CHIMAERAS

Who are the Chimaeras?

This male Elephant Fish displays the characteristic wing-shaped pectoral fins of chimaeras but the beak is unusually long. Two of its five claspers are kept within its two pelvic slits.

*L*ike sharks and rays, chimaeras have claspers and a cartilage skeleton but they occupy a different group. Unlike sharks and rays, they have a single gill opening and their upper jaw is fused to their skull just like other bony fish species. The jaw has a number of tooth plates that form a beak-like mouth under the snout. The smooth skin feels almost like that of human's to touch as it is mostly free of any rough scales or denticles and the silver-coloured body looks a bit like a polished aluminium fuselage. All chimaeras have an obvious lateral line that joins to a series of lines and canals on the face. The body is long and tapered, usually with a long fine tendril at the tip of the tail.

Where are Chimaeras Found?

*A*ll chimaeras are found in very deep water, ranging from depths of 120–1400 m on the continental slope and abyssal plain. During summer and early autumn the Elephant Fish comes into shallow coastal bays to breed; here they are caught by anglers and occasionally seen by divers. Deep-water trawlers sometimes catch quantities of these fish, which are sold under the name 'whitefish'.

This male Blackfin Ghostshark shows the two reproductive claspers and extended spiked head clasper used to hold onto the female during copulation.

What Feeds on Chimaeras?

Sharks that share the deep habitat of the chimaera are their main predators. Some, like the huge Pacific Sleeper Shark, which grows to 6 m or more, may feed on seasonally mating aggregations. A very sick Leopard Seal found resting on a beach in New Zealand had its cheek pierced by an Elephant Fish spine, providing evidence that these animals will take chimaeras if they can find them.

How do Chimaeras Produce Young?

Chimaeras are all egg-layers. The female carries tough-skinned egg cases which are dropped on the seabed. The tadpole-shaped egg cases have an assortment of ribs, membranes and filaments, depending on the species. These features are useful for lodging the eggs into crevices or entangling them onto growths or exposed reefs.

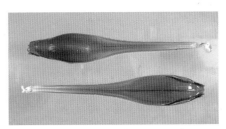

These tadpole- or flask-shaped egg cases are characteristic of chimaeras. Note the hooks at the ends.

What Defences do Chimaeras Have?

The first dorsal fin on all chimaeras has a long spine that can be raised vertically. The spine is exceptionally sharp and on some species it also has venom glands and fine serrations. Camouflage also plays a large part in a chimaera's defence, with the silver skin reflecting the available light and effectively blending in to the surrounding territory. Some chimaeras are black or brown which makes them nearly invisible in the deep abyssal plains where they live. The lateral lines on the face and body may also warn of approaching predators.

CLASPER CLUSTERS

All males have a set of five, instead of the usual two, claspers. Like sharks and rays there are two claspers behind the pelvic fins used for mating. In front of the pelvic fins are two slits in which two more retractable claspers can be found. It is assumed that these claspers, usually studded with bristles and spikes, are used to hold and align the female. On the forehead is the fifth clasper (see photo), which, when not in use, is folded down flush in a fitted hollow. The bulbous tip is covered in short spikes to enable the male to hold onto the female's pectoral fins while mating.

Elephant Fish

A silvery male Elephant Fish forages over sandy patches en route to its shallow breeding grounds.

The Elephant Fish must be the most spectacular of all the cartilaginous fish. When viewed from below, the skin is silvery white like aluminium foil but when viewed from above it has a disruptive pattern of large brown blotches and bands. It has two dorsal fins — the rear one being by far the smaller — and a long, elegant tapering tail that is used mainly as a rudder.

Its most distinctive feature is a plough-shaped nose that is used to search for food on the seabed. The end of the flexible snout is covered in sensory pores that detect movement and weak electrical currents. Behind and close to the snout is a small mouth with crushing plates. The eyes are large and set high on the head, while the face of this chimaera is traced with a map of sensory mucus-filled canals. The single gill opening is immediately in front of each large sculptured pectoral fin. It is the pectoral fins that supply the animal's primary means of locomotion.

Annual Migrations and Defence

Males and females migrate from 200 m depths offshore to enter shallow coastal bays in spring and summer to breed. Here, females drop their golden-coloured egg cases, which hatch eight months later.

Besides being well camouflaged, an Elephant Fish can defend itself with its long serrated spine that is situated just in front of the first large dorsal fin.

STARTLING EYES

Elephant Fish often have green eyes, like other chimaera species and deep-water sharks. When they are caught and hauled to the surface from great depths their eyes would not have yet reacted to the surface light and are still a startling metallic green.

Shortnose Chimaeras and Spookfish

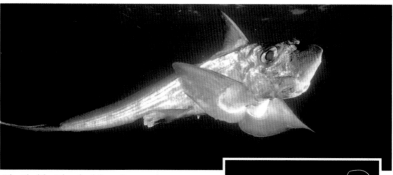

*The Blackfin Ghostshark has a large eye to accommo-
date its deep-water habitat and a Spookfish (inset)
shows its long snout with additional sensory organs.*

*I*n Australian waters there are nine
species of shortnose chimaeras and
three spookfish species. Very little is known
about the lives of these chimaeras and even less of spookfish. Swimmers or
amateur anglers would not see one of these animals but some are commercial
species and they may be found at times in southern fish markets.

Australian deep-sea chimaeras live at depths of 120–1400 m on the continental slope and abyssal plains where they feed on small fish and squid. All share
a similar body structure with smooth scaleless skin, a rounded rabbit-like head
with luminous green eyes, large pectoral fins, a single pair of gill openings,
pelvic fins, a high first dorsal fin with a single spine, a low second dorsal fin
along the back and a small leaf-shaped tail bearing a long filament.

NAMES WITH MEANING

The name 'chimaera' comes
from a legendary goat-
shaped monster in Greek
mythology that spouted fire
and in the English language
refers to something that is
beyond belief or wildly fanci-
ful. Some chimaeras belong
to the genus *Hydrolagus*,
which translates as water
hare or rabbit, an allusion to
their rabbit-like faces.

Spookfish

Spookfish have a similar body structure to
these chimaeras but they also sport a long spear-
shaped snout. The snout has sensory mucus-
filled canals and pits on the underside that help
the spookfish locate their prey. They eat shelled
invertebrates and crustaceans, such as crabs,
which are crushed in their beak-like mouths.

Spookfish live in very deep water, from depths
of 700-1700 m. In other areas of their global
distribution they have been trawled from
depths as great as 2600 m. Males have typical
chimaera-like clasper arrays and females lay
large ribbed tadpole-shaped eggs with wide
membranes on the side.

A Checklist Of Australian Sharks, Rays and Chimaeras

Listed below are the major families of sharks, rays and chimaeras that inhabit Australian waters. Only species featured in this book are included.

SHARKS

FAMILY HEXANCHIDAE
(Six and Seven Gilled Sharks)

Bluntnose Sixgill Shark *Hexanchus griseus*
Broadnose Sixgill Shark *Notorynchus cepedianus*

FAMILY ECHINORHINIDAE (Bramble Sharks)

Bramble Shark *Echinorhinus brucus*
Prickly Shark *Echinorhinus cookei*

FAMILY SQUALIDAE (Dogfish)

Brier Shark *Deania calcea*
Pygmy Shark *Euprotomicrus bispinatus*
Cookie-cutter Shark *Isistius brasiliensis*
Pacific Sleeper Shark *Somniosus pacificus*
Smalleye Pygmy Shark *Squaliolus aliae*
White-Spotted Spurdog *Squalus acanthias*

FAMILY OXYNOTIDAE (Prickly Dogfish)

Prickly Dogfish *Oxynotus bruniensis*

FAMILY PRISTIOPHORIDAE (Sawsharks)

Common Sawshark *Pristiophorus cirratus*
Southern Sawshark *Pristiophorus nudipinnis*

FAMILY HETERODONTIDAE (Horn Sharks)

Crested Horn Shark *Heterodontus galeatus*
Port Jackson Shark *Heterodontus portusjacksoni*

FAMILY PARASCYLLIIDAE
(Collared Carpet Sharks)

Rusty Carpet Shark *Parascyllium ferrugineum*
Varied Carpet Shark *Parascyllium variolatum*

FAMILY BRACHAELURIDAE (Blind Sharks)

Blind Shark *Brachaelurus waddi*

FAMILY ORECTOLOBIDAE (Wobbegongs)

Tasselled Wobbegong *Eucrossorhinus dasypogon*
Spotted Wobbegong *Orectolobus maculatus*
Ornate Wobbegong *Orectolobus ornatus*
Northern Wobbegong *Orectolobus wardi*
Cobbler Wobbegong *Sutorectus tentaculatus*

FAMILY HEMISCYLLIIDAE
(Longtail Carpet Sharks)

Grey Carpet Shark *Chiloscyllium punctatum*
Epaulette Shark *Hemiscyllium ocellatum*
Speckled Carpet Shark *Hemiscyllium trispeculare*

FAMILY STEGOSTOMATIDAE (Zebra Sharks)

Zebra Shark *Stegostoma fasciatum*

FAMILY GINGLYMOSTOMATIDAE
(Nurse Sharks)

Tawny Nurse Shark *Nebrius ferrugineus*

FAMILY RHINCODONTIDAE
(Whale Sharks)

Whale Shark *Rhincodon typus*

FAMILY ODONTASPIDIDAE
(Grey Nurse Sharks)

Grey Nurse Shark *Carcharias taurus*
Sand Tiger Shark *Odontaspis ferox*

FAMILY MITSUKURINIDAE (Goblin Sharks)

Goblin Shark *Mitsukurina owstoni*

FAMILY ALOPIIDAE (Thresher Sharks)

Pelagic Thresher Shark *Alopias pelagicus*
Bigeye Thresher Shark *Alopias superciliosus*
Thresher Shark *Alopias vulpinus*

FAMILY CETORHINIDAE (Basking Sharks)

Basking Shark *Cetorhinus maximus*

FAMILY LAMNIDAE (Mackerel Sharks)

Great White Shark *Carcharodon carcharias*
Shortfin Mako Shark *Isurus oxyrinchus*
Porbeagle Shark *Lamna nasus*

FAMILY SCYLIORHINIDAE (Catsharks)

Grey Spotted Catshark *Asymbolus analis*
Draughtboard Shark *Cephaloscyllium laticeps*